Dedication

In memory of Clarence & Bonnie,
my parents who let me go and give my heart to the world.
And dedicated to Wayne and Angela,
my siblings who encouraged me to go.
And to Ken, my soulmate
who took me with him!

Cover design by Ken Dornhecker

Travelers Together

By Becky Dornhecker

Contents

Mr. Gorbachev, tear down this wall!
—President Ronald Reagan

~1~
The Wall That Finally Fell

We sat in our compartment on the train barreling across Germany toward Berlin—toward the East. As I looked out on the villages, fields, and cities of Germany, I was surprised to realize I felt a little trepidation at the thought of entering what only one year ago had been another country—a closed, cold Communist country called East Germany.

I recalled grainy, black and white film footage I had seen as a small child of a wall being built in a city far away. I asked my mom what they were doing and she had told me they were building a wall to keep people from going from one part of the city to the other. And then she told me the part that I'm sure was the reason I never forgot that image: *Some families are even being separated by that wall!* I was horrified and could not imagine never seeing members of my family again.

But it was a very real part of recent history. The wall became a solid barrier separating people, friends, family, and a country on August 13, 1961 and wasn't torn down until the fateful night of November 9, 1989, when people scrambled on top of it with sledge hammers and started the demolition process themselves.

As our train crossed over a certain point in our journey,

my husband Ken remarked, "We're now in what used to be East Germany." As I looked out on the vast expanse of fields we were passing by, I felt the coldness and isolation that was part of this region in the not-so-distant past.

As we were approaching Berlin, we had to stop and change trains. Ken told me that during the communist reign, guards with machine guns would probably have boarded and checked our identifications. For people traveling out of Berlin, there would have been dogs sent under trains to sniff out people hiding in the undercarriages of the cars. But now with the wall down, it was a routine change to another train for us.

But there was a disparity. We were now on a former East German train and the difference was glaring. Where before we had traveled in clean, soft-cushioned seats, we were now seated on hard, plastic benches. The interior of the train was grubby and unappealing. Even though much had changed on the outside, eastern Germany still had a long way to go to catch up with its refined and sophisticated neighbor.

The year was 1990 and the wall had been down less than a year. I had married my husband, Ken, seven months before and he was eager to show me this great love of his life.

Only about a year after becoming a Christian, he had felt the call to be an evangelist. That calling meant he didn't just preach inside the walls of the church. The evangelist is called by God to take the gospel out where people live their everyday life and tell them about Jesus. If there are people anywhere on planet earth that have not heard the message of salvation, the evangelist cannot be satisfied until they have. That meant for me, we would be doing plenty of traveling together and a lot of our ministry would be outside the walls of the church.

Ken had gone to Bible school in 1983 and when he graduated an opportunity arose for him to go to Wiesbaden, Germany for 18 months with Teen Challenge—a ministry whose function was reaching lost, troubled people through street evangelism. This was a perfect fit for him—mission work and evangelism. Once his 18 months were up with Teen Challenge, he spent most of his time in Germany and in other countries of the world as a Missionary Evangelist.

We even met each other because of his mission work. I was working with a ministry that sent books, cassette tapes, and letters each month to missionaries in foreign lands. Ken *got on my list* while he was living in Germany and we began corresponding with each other. He was from the same area in Texas I was living, so when he came home we eventually met.

At times, I was even a little jealous when he would talk about Germany. God had called him to this land and he was passionate and zealous about ministering here. He would talk about Germany like someone talking about a person very dear to their heart. I was excited to be finally sharing this part of my husband with him.

When Ken had lived in Germany, the country was separated into two countries. At the end of World War II, the Soviet Union army had advanced into Germany and had taken over almost half of the land, including the capital, Berlin. When the allied forces (U.S., United Kingdom, France, and the Soviet Union) divided the country into sectors, the Soviet Union kept the land they had acquired. The post-war agreement called for the four powers to control the German capital. The only problem was that Berlin was right in the middle of what was now Soviet-controlled land.

The solution was to divide Berlin into two sections. The result was West Berlin became an island of freedom in the middle of communist East Germany. The people of West Berlin could travel freely anywhere they wanted to go, by plane or train. But the people of East Berlin lived in a suppressed, communistic city.

When people from the Eastern part of Berlin and even the Eastern-bloc countries around Germany started using this fluid border to escape the repressions coming down from the Soviet Union, the leaders had to do something. Three and a half million people defected from the country of East Germany, using the door left open in West Berlin. They were losing all their elite, educated people and they intended to stop them from leaving.

The first wall that went up around West Berlin was made of barbed wire and was manned by guards with machine guns. The more permanent wall was then built. It was actually two walls, one enclosing the people of East Berlin and the second wall around 100 yards away on the West Berlin border. In between these walls was no man's land, a big swath of ground left open for guards in East Berlin to catch people trying to escape. They also had a good shot of these people from their guard towers and many people were killed trying to reach freedom.

Now, because of the reunification of East and West Germany, Ken's ministry area had greatly increased! The reunification had been signed just two months before we arrived. We wanted to check out the new freedom to travel unhindered anywhere in this land.

We settled with some friends in Berlin and then Ken took me around the city to show me some of the areas he had been to in his ministry to Germany. As we approached Checkpoint Charlie, he again told me some of the stories he had experienced in his many times *across the wall*.

When the wall around West Berlin went up, there were places or checkpoints where the allied forces from the west could pass through to the east. The most famous checkpoint was in the American sector called *Checkpoint Charlie.*

Ten years after the wall went up, the East began to allow West Germany visitors to also pass through these checkpoints. But only one way—people from the east were not allowed to cross. Ken came to Berlin often and would cross the line between West and East here at Checkpoint Charlie. He had a network of friends and Christians that he would minister with as they evangelized the best they could. He spent the day with them, doing as much as possible to give out tracts and witness to people.

One of their ploys was to start handing out tracts on the platform just as the trains approached. After they had given out as many as they could in these few seconds, they would jump on the train before the doors closed and go to the next station, trying to stay one step ahead of the *stasi* (secret police).

As an American, Ken regarded it as a game of cat and mouse, but looking back he realizes how very serious it was for the East German young people he was working with. If they had been caught it could even have meant jail time.

On the occasions when he was stopped by the *stasi*, they would reveal that they knew all his whereabouts for his time spent in East Berlin. My thought when I heard this was why would a government spend that much time and money following around a young guy and his friends? It still is beyond me the energy they expended on keeping their thumbs on people.

But that was all part of the mindset of this repressive nation. And it is incredible, but it was very, very serious. Ken was reminded of this on one of his trips to the east. He was probably a bit naïve as an American who was used to freedom and had the safety and backing of an American passport. But on one occasion, he realized how quickly that security can be taken away.

When he crossed the border, he knew he could only stay for a 24-hour period. In other words, he always had to be out by midnight. He had to exchange a certain amount of his West German *Deutschemarks* (currency) for East German *Marks*. The exchange rate was very unfair and the East German money could never be changed back at the end of the day (and there was very little to buy, even in restaurants). He also had to pay for an East German "visa."

Ken went across the wall on several occasions and I'm sure was a great encouragement to the Christians in East Germany. But on one night, he pushed his visit right up to just enough time left to walk to the border and get across.

As he was hurrying toward the checkpoint, a uniformed man suddenly stepped out in front of him. He brusquely asked for Ken's passport and he handed it over to this stranger. Before Ken knew what was going on, the man had disappeared around a corner. It took a few seconds for Ken to realize what had just happened. He was now in East Germany, and without the American passport, just like any other young man in this country. He felt suffocated and trapped, now surrounded by barbed wire and controlled by guards with vicious dogs and machine guns.

As the minutes passed, and the man had still not returned with his passport, he began to earnestly and urgently pray! Finally, after fifteen anxious minutes, the man returned and handed him back the precious document. He made it out of the country just minutes before midnight.

As we stood there at Checkpoint Charlie, Ken also told me about being harassed in the buildings just on the other side. The guards would single him out, take him to a small enclosed room, and have him empty his pockets. They would intimidate as much as they dared, sometimes questioning him over and over, and leaving him alone for long stretches of time. It was all a well-organized plot of mind-games and intimidation.

But he also told me about his very last visit across the wall. As he was coming back through Checkpoint Charlie to the west, he was motioned to step out of the line and to follow a guard to be interrogated. When he and the guard were alone in the room, the guard asked Ken to take everything out of his pockets. Ken had done this on many occasions, so went through the familiar process.

The guard looked down at the pocket New Testament Ken had placed on the table and touched it briefly, almost caressing it. He looked at Ken and said softly, "A wonderful book." Nothing more was said, but it showed Ken that many of these men were just doing a job—maybe even one they didn't truly believe in. He didn't realize it at the time, but this man turned out to be the last East German guard he ever dealt with.

We now walked through Checkpoint Charlie with ease, with no one stopping us. It was just another city street now. As we started walking toward the buildings which used to be the East Germany side, we noticed trash everywhere. As we drew closer and peeked into the buildings that were some of the *stasi* headquarters, we saw what had become of these elite structures.

The people of East Berlin had taken their anger and frustration out on these symbols of oppression. In their new-found freedom, they had come in and trashed the buildings—tearing down parts of them and making them unusable for any further occupation. We walked through rooms that Ken remembered and saw the devastation firsthand. Many, many memories came back to him and we contemplated the freedom that his friends from the East now enjoyed.

Right after we left Germany, we learned that the whole area around Checkpoint Charlie had been bulldozed to the ground. The site now houses sleek new office buildings and shops. But one thing still remains—the museum housing info about all the ingenious ways people used to escape the communist regime, like cars that people had hidden in and even part of a hot air balloon. It also told the story of people who lost their lives trying to simply get from one side of a city to the other...just trying to rejoin their family members—sometimes spouses or children.

Ken tried to show me as much of his beloved Germany as we could fit into our two weeks. We headquartered with some friends in Wiesbaden, the city he had lived in. From there we traveled by train to different parts of Germany, including Berlin and down south to Berchtesgaden.

On our way to Berchtesgaden, we only had about ten minutes to change trains in Munich. We had to run with our suitcases toward the gate for the train. This was the last train that day and we knew if we didn't catch this one, we would lose our reservation in Berchtesgaden.

As we rounded the corner where the train should have been, there was no train. Ken looked down about 100 yards and said "Oh no! The train is outside the station on a side track and is far away. We'll have to run for it."

He took off down the dirt path to the train and I followed...for a while. Our suitcases back then were made completely different than they are today. They had wheels, but only about the size of quarters on each corner. The luggage was pulled by a strap on the side. If you were lucky and on pretty smooth pavement, it would not tip over, but even that didn't always hold true.

I was hurrying as fast as I could, but on the dirt, the wheels were useless. We didn't pack very smart in those days, so I picked up the heavy suitcase and started running behind Ken. After about 50 yards, I sat everything down and stood there to catch my breath.

Ken was at the train and I could see the conductor standing with his whistle ready, waiting for us. Ken turned around, expecting to see me right behind him. He waved for me to come on and put one foot on the train. I was thinking what a nice man the conductor was to wait on me like that. They were very proud of being punctual and didn't like their trains to be late. But Ken told me later the only reason he wasn't blowing his whistle for the train to leave was because Ken had one foot on the ground and one foot on the train! He was actually very angry with him.

I could see the whole train was waiting on me so I picked up my suitcase again and finally made it to the train. We boarded and then found out that the train was completely packed. I sat with the luggage in the small area that connects the wagons together and Ken went in search of a seat. We had to sit in the aisle on small fold-down seats for most of the journey, but we were on our way!

As we rode the train to this mountain village, we started seeing the Alps long before arriving in Berchtesgaden. It was a beautiful ride as we chugged up the last miles on the local train we had caught in Salzburg, Austria. The village opened up like a scenic painting with a clear mountain river flowing right through the middle. I felt I was in wonderland as we found a hotel right beside the river and at the foot of the most beautiful snow-capped mountains I had ever seen.

We went for a boat ride on Lake Königssee, which was situated between mountains and is known for its emerald green color. As we rode along the quiet waters of this beautiful lake, we came upon a church out in the middle of nowhere. St. Bartholomew's church was first built in 1134 as a chapel. In 1694 it was rebuilt with its distinctive red onion domed roof.

The boat let us off here to tour the church and then to return at our leisure on one of the other scheduled boats. It was a beautiful, solitary place and we learned more about the history. The only way to get to it was either by boat or by pilgrimage over the mountains called *Steinernes Meer* (Sea of Rocks). It is said that the pilgrimage began in 1635 when the citizens of Salzburg wanted to give thanks to God for saving them from the plague. There is still a Catholic pilgrimage to this out of the way spot every August, beginning in Austria across the mountains. After Berchtesgaden became part of Bavaria in 1810, the church was used as a hunting lodge for the kings of Bavaria.

While in Berchtesgaden, we also visited Eagle's Nest. This was one of the infamous special hangouts for Hitler during the war. He had a house on one of the mountaintops that he called Eagle's Nest. We rode a bus four miles around switch-back curves up the side of the mountain. We then came to a parking lot where they ushered us into a cave-like structure in the side of the mountain. We walked through a long tunnel, with the walls and floors so cold they were damp with moisture.

There we rode an elevator 400 feet up through the mountain to the place Hitler would go with his cohorts and military men. The elevator carried us to the center of the house. As the doors opened, we were in the house we had seen on documentaries and news stories. There are several famous pictures and films of Hitler on the deck and inside this mountain vacation home.

We had picked a clear day and could see the beautiful snow-capped mountains all around us. It was truly breathtaking. While we were there, we had lunch on the terrace overlooking Salzburg, Austria.

But as we toured the place where we knew Hitler had been and probably planned some of his war strategies, I thought back to his ultimate end. He had much of what the world considers important—fame, power, money, even a mountain-top retreat. But he was probably one of the most hated men that ever lived. He died by suicide in a bunker underground as the allies closed in on him to stop his tyranny.

While we were on this trip, Ken preached some in churches and a Bible school, but we also made plans with his friend in Berlin to ship our tent to Germany for crusades the following year. We were assured by his friend that he would take care of all the arrangements on the German end. Several months before summer, we packed our big 500-seat blue and white tent and sent it across the ocean to Europe. It turned out to be a lesson in changing plans mid-stream and flowing with the ups and downs that sometimes comes with missionary work.

Something hidden. Go and find it.
Go and look behind the Ranges—
Something lost behind the Ranges.
Lost and waiting for you. Go!
—Rudyard Kipling

~2~
New Beginnings for a Vanished Country

We heard the service announcement over the intercom. Our flight was delayed! When they started giving us vouchers for food, we realized this would not be a short delay, but it would be hours. A service truck had run into our plane on the tarmac and it was being "repaired!"

We were stuck at Dulles International Airport in Washington D.C., on our way to Berlin. I was leading a team of five other people, two of which this was their very first flight…ever. Ken had left for Berlin almost three weeks before to get the crusades set up. We had shipped our tent months ago and Ken had picked it up at the port in Hamburg. Everything seemed ready to go, if only we could just get there.

After a five-hour delay, we were finally on our way to London. We would transfer there on to Berlin. But because of our long delay in Washington, we missed this transfer. After another agonizing wait in London, we finally landed in Berlin 23 hours later.

Ken was at the airport to meet us and took us to a hostel in Oranienburg, in the former country of East Germany. The Sachsenhausen Concentration Camp had been located here, and Ken pointed out the train station where Corrie Ten Boom (of *The Hiding Place* book and movie) disembarked to march to the Camp. It became a training facility for SS officers and knew no bounds in cruelty and brutality. Thousands died just of starvation and disease, much less all those who were deliberately murdered by this heartless regime.

Upon arriving at the hostel, we divided up in our dorm-room type accommodations—girls in one room and guys in another. Even with exhaustion, I didn't sleep very well since my body had not adjusted to the time difference. We went downstairs the next morning, though, to a lovely German breakfast of meat, cheese, bread, jams, and boiled *wurst* that looked like foot-long hotdogs. It all tasted wonderful and we grew accustomed to these huge spreads of food each morning.

As we were shown around the premises the first day, we realized it was spread out like a campground. The buildings were all old and were being updated even during our time there. The showers were in another building from the rooms. As we checked out the shower, we had to go down steps into what looked like a cellar, which was a little creepy.

The shower was a huge open room with showerheads hanging down from the ceiling and was turned on from a chain hanging down. It reminded me of the stories I had heard about the showers of the concentration camps that were really gas chambers. I knew different, but it still gave me something to think about as I reached up to turn on the water.

As we began to settle in our new home for the next two

weeks, we learned that our plans for the tent crusades were not going to work out. We had been told everything on this end was taken care of, but it was not. The bureaucracy of Germany would not let us set up a tent that did not have their specifications. And their specifications were the size of a telephone book! We were very disappointed but our team were troopers and we went on to Plan B.

We were working with an American friend of Ken's in Berlin that he had met while in Guatemala years before. We were also connected with a couple, Frank and Lisa, who had grown up under the communist rule of East Germany. They had a small church in Berlin and were coming alongside to help us.

Frank had been imprisoned by the *stasi* of East Germany while trying to escape to the West. At that time, the West had a policy of "buying" these young people out of prison and settling them in the West. This had happened to Frank after several horrible years in prison. Once he and Lisa married, they went on a quest to India, searching for truth. They found **the truth** from a missionary in India, who told them about Jesus. They came back to Germany and Frank began pastoring a church.

We visited Frank's church several times and learned another fact about the fall of communism we didn't know. The Soviet Union had thousands of their troops in East Germany before the wall came down. With this sudden change in geographical lines, they didn't have the funds to relocate them back to the Soviet Union all at once. These troops were stuck in the country of Germany until they were all finally brought home in 1994. Some of these Russian soldiers were members of Frank's church and we were able to meet them.

Frank would arrive at our hostel every morning and say with enthusiasm and vigor, "Come, we make something! Yes?" He also had a heart for evangelism and would lead us as we went out witnessing and preaching.

Frank's father and mother lived in Oranienburg, and they welcomed our team to their home. We spent a lot of time with them and affectionately called them Mutti and Poppi. They would serve us lunch on their patio and we would listen as they talked about the years they had spent as citizens of East Germany and their newfound freedom.

Poppi told us that they literally had their bags packed since 1954, but were reluctant to leave. This was their home and they kept thinking things would get better. He told us that Mutti had felt they needed to leave, but he kept hesitating—till it was too late! Everything changed overnight in 1961. The wall was up all around this country and no one was allowed to leave.

He told us that the *stasi* had control over everything, even the conversation in one's home. He said there were microphones and cameras hidden in people's homes. And one of their insidious tactics was for the kindergarten teachers to listen in on the children's conversations, then report the parents if things were said against the government in any way. One out of every 6 people of the population was an informer, many times a neighbor or even a friend.

If anyone had a company with more than five employees, the party would take their business away because they were making too much money. And only one out of four were educated and these were people who had passed tests showing they knew much about Stalin, Lenin, and the communist party. In other words, only party members were allowed an education.

He told us the Germans in this new country were just as smart as their neighbors to the West and knew how to make good cars (like Mercedes and BMW), but were only allowed to produce the *Trabant (Trabbi)*. To own one, a person would order one and pay for it, then wait up to seven years for it to arrive!

We saw these cars on the streets while in Berlin and even up close with one that had been wrecked at Poppi's house. They were made of what looked and felt like pressed wood fiber board and we could break off pieces with our hands. They were actually made of something called Duroplast, a hard plastic made from recycled materials. The engine sounded like a lawn mower going down the street. They looked so unsafe, now traveling the highways with the larger and faster cars made in the West.

Poppi told us about the antenna boxes people would make for TVs, so they could pick up Western television. People began to see the demand for them and started making them to sell. They became so popular that the *stasi* actually started making and selling them! They were making money under-the-table from products that they themselves had deemed illegal!

It was eye-opening to talk at length to people who had walked through the ordeal of their country being closed off to the rest of the world. We also learned that throughout this time, Poppi had not been a Christian. He told us his heart had been hard, like a Panzer tank. He had only given his life to the Lord around the time the wall came down. His bright eyes and energetic ways showed us that he was now truly free!

Frank talked to his brothers and Poppi and decided that we could put up the main section of our tent on Poppi's land. We worked for hours hammering the huge stakes into the ground and getting the tent laid out on the ground like a huge patchwork quilt. Finally the time came for the center pole to go up and with a heave, the men raised the tent up! What a sight it was, to see the tent finally raised on German soil.

As the work went on that afternoon, we heard a noise that was getting closer and closer. Someone else had noticed the tent being raised. We looked up to see Russian *Hind* helicopters buzzing us. The whole time the tent was up, we were visited by these helicopters, keeping a close eye on us!

We had seen much evidence in our time in the East to know that just because the country was now part of West Germany, there were still many old-time party members still in charge, especially on the local level. I'm sure they did not like the changes that had come and still wanted to exert their authority and power. We weren't sure why those in charge were checking us out, but I'm sure they wanted us to know that they knew what we were doing!

We held a few meetings in the tent, but it wasn't as well attended as it could have been if we had been able to set up in a city center. When our time was up in Germany, we decided to leave the tent there. The last we heard, it was shipped to the Soviet Union where there were fewer restrictions. We have prayed over the years that God used it to bring many souls to His kingdom.

Even though the crusades in the tent did not work out the way we had thought, God opened other avenues of ministry. One of these was a small church in a village deep into the former East called Booch. It was one of the most beautiful rides of our trip. We went through tree-covered lanes and fields of blowing wheat and grass, through village after village of this country where time had seemed to stand still for over three decades. At one point, our guide pointed out that the trees we could see in the near distance were actually in Poland, only a kilometer away.

We arrived at the pastor's house, deep in the forgotten forests near the Polish border. As we sat in their living room drinking hot coffee, we could see deer roaming the woods beyond. It was an enchanting place. And it became even more special when Ken was able to minister in their church and people were saved that night!

Another way we were able to minister with Frank was something very dear to Ken's heart—preaching out on the street, where the people were. On one occasion, Frank was preaching on the sidewalk when all of a sudden he was drenched with water! We all looked up and a woman from an upstairs window had thrown her tub of dirty dish water on top of him. Naturally it took him a few seconds to recover from the shock, then he looked up and very deliberately said to the lady, "I love you, in Jesus" and continued to preach.

This had quite an effect on the crowd. Where before they had been slightly disinterested, they now were galvanized against the woman in the window and were eager to hear what Frank was saying. Ken and I were able to lead a couple of people to Jesus as we talked with those in the crowd when Frank finished. We preached several more times on the street and once at a park filled with American students from the nearby JFK High School.

While we were still at the hostel, an amazing thing happened. We were outside one day and noticed a group of young kids arrive for a holiday. We befriended them and soon had a mini-vacation Bible school going on in the small courtyard. One of our team had a guitar and led them in some songs. Ken then preached a simple message of the gospel to them and 19 of the 21 raised their hands to receive Jesus. We spent some more time with these new converts and gave them booklets in German. It was an unexpected gift for us to be able to minister to these kids.

After a couple of weeks, most of our team headed back to the States. We were so grateful that they had flowed with us through all the changes.

Ken and I remained in Germany and were on a train, headed out to another small village called Radis in the former East just below Berlin. In the time Ken had been in Germany before I arrived, he had been seeking God about us moving to Germany for a time and holding crusades. He had a contact with a pastor and we were on our way to visit him.

The train began to slow and the conductor announced that we were at the Radis stop. As the door to the train opened, we looked out and saw…nothing. No station, no platform. We knew we didn't have long to contemplate, so we pulled our luggage off and stepped into the dirt and scraggly weeds beside the tracks.

It was the loneliest feeling, watching that train pull away and go on down the tracks. Was this actually our destination? We could see some buildings in the distance and realized this was indeed Radis. We started walking and soon came to the small village. We found our way to the pastor's house and settled into the lovely loft room they had prepared for us. It looked like a doll house, and in the German way, there were cookies and fruit juice laid out for us.

We had scheduled a few days to spend here and we began to get to know our hosts. We were eager to work with the few German churches wanting to evangelize this former communist stronghold. We thought we could occasionally help this pastor with crusades but his expectation seemed to be that he wanted us to live and work exclusively in their small village church.

Ken had to do most of the talking for us since neither the pastor nor his wife spoke English. From the beginning, there seemed to be misunderstandings. From an early age in my Christian walk, I have relied on God's peace to lead me in decision making. A verse from Colossians had become one of my life verses: "And let the peace from Christ rule (act as umpire continually) in your hearts, deciding and settling with finality all questions that arise in your minds" (Colossians 3:15a AMP).

But God's peace was definitely not in either of our hearts and we felt pressure to make a quick decision on something that would completely change our lives. We also just didn't seem to have the same vision as the pastor and finally told him no, that we would not be moving to Radis.

While we were in this part of the country, we decided to stop in Wittenberg, the home of the University of Wittenberg, established in 1502. A young Catholic priest by the name of Martin Luther was a professor here in 1508. On October 31, 1517, Luther nailed his *95 Theses* (against the selling of indulgences for canceling sin) on the door of the *All Saints Church* and the Protestant Reformation was begun. Even though the original door was destroyed by fire centuries ago, we were able to stand before the replacement put there in 1857.

Our time in Germany was coming to a close. It is a huge mission field with less than 2% evangelical Christians. For this journey, we had explored and ministered mainly in the newly opened-up East. It was a pivotal time as people poured into the area to offer them all the things they had been missing—from new cars to new religions. We couldn't find good toilet paper while in the East, but we saw new Mercedes cars for sale in empty fields. We also saw Hare Krishnas and cults in the airport.

There was so much change going on—both good and bad. Glamor, opulence, greed, and porn also poured across the border. Nothing was held back and the East German people were inundated with all the world had to offer after almost 40 years of suppression.

There was also high unemployment with all the changes. Under communism, most people had a job, even if it was at minimum wage and 10 people doing the job that one could do. It must have been mind-numbingly boring. But we actually saw t-shirts that said, "I want my wall back" because of the unemployment.

Now it was part of our mission field—the whole Germany. We were ready for the challenge and eagerly added the freedom to preach to our agenda. We knew the change they really needed was Jesus. We would be back!

Afraid? Of what?
Afraid to see the Saviour's face,
To hear His welcome, and to trace,
The glory gleam from wounds of grace,
Afraid? Of that?
—E. H. Hamilton

~3~
A Call in the Night

The call came during the middle of the night, like all his telephone calls had been. I reached for the phone in anticipation, but instantly could tell by the tone of Ken's voice, that something was wrong.

Most of our phone calls were filled with the good news of people being saved. The only telephones in the country were in government buildings, like post offices. So when Ken wanted to call me, he had to go to the post office at a certain time of day, and stand in a long line. He had no other choice. And that certain time of day happened to be around 3:00 am in Texas.

The year was 1991 and Ken was far away in the Balkan nation of Albania. It had been the country that was considered the most closed and fanatical of all the communist countries. In early 1991 Communism had finally given way and the country was poised for restructuring like the Soviet Union had experienced. But for now it was a Wild West scenario. Freedom in the midst of corruption and mind-sets that was still very much communist.

Ken and his pastor friend, Al, had sat at our kitchen table months ago and planned this trip. As they dreamed and schemed with a calendar and map of all the places they wanted to go, they sketched an itinerary of 40 days! I looked at my still newly-wed husband to see if he would balk at this, but he was excitedly running with it. I could understand his passion and drive for missions, but really felt 40 days would be a huge test for me.

When on the field, the days seem to fly by, but when waiting back home, the hours seem to creep along like waiting for Christmas as a six year old! I took little comfort in the fact that even on their plane ride across the ocean, they looked at one another and said, *What have we done? We're going away from our wives for 40 days!*

When they arrived in Albania, they found a land frozen in time. There were few cars and they were more likely to see carts being pulled by horses. It was almost like they had landed on a movie set, depicting time from the early 1900s. Each day their host took their American dollars and went searching for food. He would come back after hours of searching, maybe with a side of lamb on his shoulder. They would eat from this for a few days, and since no refrigeration was available, the carcass was simply wrapped in cloth on the sink drain board.

Ken and Al had taken processed foods, like macaroni and cheese, and they shared these with their host family. (Ken found out later they thought that was all Americans ate— food from boxes. But they were thankful for the items Ken and Al brought with them. They had been worried they would not have enough food to feed them each day.) There was little in the form of our modern conveniences, and if they wanted hot water to bathe in, it had to be heated on the small hotplate.

The irony of this closed nation was not lost on Ken when he learned that the people were fed constant communist propaganda and were told they were better off than the rest of the world. That's why they had be to so closed and separated from everyone else. If people found out how good they lived, then everyone would want their way of life. Their ugly block apartments were called palaces. The people of Albania had no idea they were being deceived on such a grand scale.

But the government began to fall, just like all the other communist-bloc countries in the early nineties. The people were much like baby birds with their mouths wide open, experiencing change like they had never thought possible. My husband and his friend wanted to be part of bringing the wonderful gospel of Jesus to that land at this strategic time.

It was monumental and Ken was almost giddy when he would talk to me of sharing Jesus with people who had never heard His name. One man told Ken when he asked the man if he knew Jesus, *No, I've never met anyone from Greece!* It was a ministry time that Ken had only dreamed of as they traversed across this burgeoning land to carry the gospel.

One of Ken's favorite verses is, "It has always been my ambition to preach the gospel where Christ was not known" (Romans 15:20a NIV). Because this was the most closed and isolated nation of any of the Communist countries, they truly had never heard the gospel.

Ken would laugh out loud as he told me how wonderful it was to bring Jesus to these people. When they would hold Bible studies, there were so many people trying to get in to get tracts and literature, it almost looked like a riot outside the home.

During their trip, they were able to hold meetings in an auditorium for several days. At one of these meetings, they were praying for the sick. A man brought a child for Ken to pray for and pushed the little one into Ken's arms. After that, other people began shoving and pushing to get their babies prayed over. A moment of pure pandemonium broke out, as people began rushing the stage area. Ken realized all their video and electronic equipment was at the back of the stage, but could do nothing about it for the crowd.

When all the people had been prayed for and had exited the building, Ken checked their equipment. There had been boxes of Bibles right beside the equipment. All the Bibles had been taken with the empty boxes strewn about, but all their equipment was still there.

When Ken and Al picked out a building they thought would work for their crusades, they would go to authorities, who only months before had been the elite communist party representative. When they asked for permission to hold crusades in their city buildings, some cooperated, but others made it very difficult or refused all together. But they were amazed at occurrences that took place, like when they were able to hold services in the Communist Worker's Hall!

When they would go out into villages and preach with their interpreter, they would ask for a show of hands of those who wanted to accept Jesus. They were thrilled but skeptical when the whole village would raise their hands. They would take the time to explain it all again to be sure they had understood why they were raising their hands, but the result was the same. The Albanian people had been denied this wonderful good news for years, and they would not be denied now!

As Ken and Al had prepared for the trip and sought to get visas, they were warned about going into Albania. There was no American Embassy and were even advised not to go. There would be no help for them if anything went wrong or if the country became unstable or even volatile. They would be on their own!

All this was on my mind as I heard Ken's voice that night and knew that things were not right. For one thing, he was talking in puzzling ways, telling me to read the book of David, chapter 54, but that the end (last verse) had taken place. I grabbed my Bible and began reading what I knew he meant, Psalm 54.

> [1] Save me, O God, by your name;
>   vindicate me by your might.
> [2] Hear my prayer, O God;
>   listen to the words of my mouth.

³ Arrogant foes are attacking me;
   ruthless people are trying to kill me—
   people without regard for God.
⁴ Surely God is my help;
   the Lord is the one who sustains me.
⁵ Let evil recoil on those who slander me;
   in your faithfulness destroy them.
⁶ I will sacrifice a freewill offering to you;
   I will praise your name, LORD, for it is good.
⁷ You have delivered me from all my troubles,
   and my eyes have looked in triumph on
   my foes (NIV).

Ken also told me Al's dad was sick and they needed to come home. He tried to comfort me that everything was ok, but it was all so confusing. I hung up from Ken fully awake and in prayer mode. Even though it was the middle of the night, I called other people to pray. I felt like Ken was in some kind of danger that he wasn't telling me.

Later that night, I got a call from Al's wife who explained all the codes they were using. Because this was a country that had just come from under the treacherous and inscrutable reign of communism, they realized things could become dicey at any moment. They figured the telephone lines were still tapped, so before Al left they had settled on phrases they would use if Al and Ken were in trouble.

If they needed help in getting out of the country, they would say Al's dad had died. If something had happened but they were ok, they would say Al's dad was sick. She tried to reassure me that they must be ok, since Al had used the second coded phrase. But I knew they were still in Albania, and I had no idea what had happened to bring them to this point of fleeing the country ten days early!

After a long and sleepless night and another day of not knowing what was going on, I finally got the call I had been desperately waiting on. Ken was in Switzerland. He was safe! And then he started explaining the whole situation.

Ken, Al, their host and their interpreter had rented one of the few cars in Albania and driven to the southern part of the country. They had been warned by people that they should not be out after dark. As they started home that day, they realized the hours had passed and it would be dark before they arrived back in Elbasan. As they went through the small villages, they drove carefully, often going around herds of sheep or horse-drawn carts.

But in one village, they came across something strange. It was around sunset, and there were huge rocks across the road and a gang of men standing around them. As they approached, they were motioned over to the side of the road. Instantly, everyone in the car knew something wasn't right. For one thing the men were all holding large rocks in their hands. They also remembered that just the week before, in another part of Albania, several people had been killed by thieves wanting their cars. Life seemed to be cheap in this country experiencing such newfound freedoms.

As they slowed the car to the side of the road and realized the danger, the host started shouting, *Ik! Ik! Ik!* (Go! Go! Go!). The driver popped the clutch and took off, going back onto the road. As he did, one man had already grabbed the door handle next to Ken. Ken had reached up and slammed the lock down just in time. But as the car gathered speed, the assailant – looking Ken straight in the eye – would not let go. Ken watched the determined man as his hold on the handle was finally jerked loose and he started summersaulting in the air.

Another drama was playing out for the driver. One of the attackers was so determined to stop them that he jumped in front of the car and threw his hands out. Because they knew their lives were in danger, the driver continued on, hitting the man and flipping him over the top of the car before he landed in the road. Ken looked behind them as they sped off and could see he was not hurt that badly. He was sitting in the middle of the road, with his fist pumping the air in defiance of them.

They rode on into the growing darkness, not knowing if there were dozens of such villages. At each mile, those in the car were quiet, keeping an eye out for other bandits and places of entrapment. But as Ken and the rest traveled on that night to Elbasan, they also realized another kind of danger they could be in.

They had no recourse if the men had the sense to turn them in to the police and claim they were innocent bi-standers in the whole affair. The warnings that they were on their own with no U.S. Embassy in this country came back to them. They made their decision on that long ride home that night that they should leave the country as soon as possible.

The next day at some point was when Ken had called me. They were trying to get passage out of Albania at the time. They miraculously secured two seats on an outgoing flight. Later on the plane, because they were not booked officially for this flight, officials had boarded the plane and tried to figure out why their numbers did not match. But after a while, the plane finally took off and soon they were in Zurich, calling their wives.

My emotions were running the gambit, glad he was ok, but still fueled by the thoughts of *what if?* Ken was explaining to me that since they still had 10 days left before their flight to the U.S. was scheduled, they had just tried to change their tickets. They were non-refundable tickets, and could not be changed! (That was before you could pay a fee to change them.) They would have to purchase new tickets if they wanted to come home. So he and Al had decided to just stay there in Zurich for the remaining 10 days.

That hit my sleep-deprived, 30-days-away-from-my-husband, not-knowing-what-was-going-on-with-him-the-past-24-hours mind like a thunderbolt! *Hun-uh!* I said. *You're coming home! I don't care what it cost!* As he came out of the phone booth, Al immerged from another one with the same look on his face. His wife had said the same thing. They were paying for a new ticket and coming home!

It may not have ended the way they planned, but they saw hundreds if not thousands come to Jesus as they preached in theatres, gymnasiums, market squares, and in great open plazas. They preached in orthodox churches, and held baptisms in a flowing river. They discipled the new converts in simple home Bible studies. For weeks they were able to live the life that evangelists only dream of. From these beginnings, Al started a church in Elbasan that is still going today.

~4~
Opportunity of a Lifetime!

In 1993, we were given an opportunity we just couldn't pass up. Billy Graham was planning a huge outreach in Europe. The actual crusade was held in Essen, Germany, but Mr. Graham's sermon was broadcast to 1400 venues in 59 countries!

That's where we came in. We were helping with the venue in Wiesbaden, Germany. A hall was rented and hundreds of feet of cable run to receive the transmission. We would hold our own preliminaries and altar call after Mr. Graham's sermon.

It went for five nights and was called *Pro Christ*. We could hardly believe this type of outreach was happening right here in Germany, where Ken had labored for so many years.

After we arrived in Germany, we went by to get a look at the hall that had been rented. It looked like something out of a Victorian period-piece movie set—tall, ornate ceilings and walls. Our job that day was to help lay down the seemingly miles of wires and cables and tape it all to the floor.

The first night would be a test for the 1400 locations to make sure the satellite feed was working. We had the projector in place in the center aisle, and my job was to guard it and make sure no one ran into it or pushed any buttons. I learned my German phrase *Bitte nicht anfassen!* (Please do not touch!) I even had to use it later, when to my horror, some kids were running and trying to climb through the stand it was sitting on.

All of the 200-some workers at our hall grew quiet and held their breath as the time for the initial broadcast came. Were all the cables and wires hooked up right? Would the feed come through? All of a sudden, we were seeing the huge banner in Essen—*Ich Bin der Weg, die Wahrheit, und das Leben!* (I Am the Way, the Truth and the Life!) A cheer went up as we all breathed a sigh of relief.

We then heard a short message from Mr. Graham. He encouraged us all in the work we were about to do over the next few days. I could tell he was not used to speaking solely to Christian audiences and at one point appeared on the verge of giving an altar call. He seemed to catch himself and then asked us to pray and dedicate our lives to God this week.

The next five nights were wonderful. Our hall filled the first night and we had to turn away around 150 people. So we rented another hall two buildings away that would seat 100 more people. We again worked through the day to prepare the building so it would be ready for the night's meeting. We strung the wires and cables up over the adjoining five-story rooftop and down into our building.

That next night, they even mentioned the Wiesbaden venue in the preliminaries in Essen. They told how we had strung cables from one building to another so **no one would be turned away.**

The meetings from Essen were also broadcast with over 40 languages being translated. We also had an Arabic and English room set aside for these languages to be interpreted.

Even in the main hall set up for Germans, there were numerous countries represented. We befriended one young man who attended from the country of Nepal. A neighbor had brought him to the meetings. When I introduced myself and began to talk to him, he told me he wanted to know more about this religion.

Ken shared with him one evening before the meeting started and asked if he knew what the Bible was all about. He didn't, so Ken took time to explain to him that God had breathed His own spirit into the Bible—it was His words and message.

When I was talking to our new young friend, he expressed that he wanted to make money—lots of it. That seemed to be the only goal he had in his life. Later, Billy Graham preached on *what will a man give in exchange for his soul.* I prayed those words would influence him as he sought to know more about Jesus.

He came to all the services. At the end of our five days together, it was difficult to say goodbye to everyone. We exchanged addresses with our Nepalese friend and when we returned to the U.S., we sent him a Bible in his own language.

After we returned home, we heard a wonderful testimony from our friend in Wiesbaden. The director over the Wiesbaden venue, Dr. Bienic, had asked a friend of his to come to the crusade each night. His friend was a lawyer and had excuse after excuse for not attending. Finally on the last night of the crusade, he decided to come to the meeting to see what it was all about.

He walked in and sat down and listened as the preliminaries got under way. There was live music and then testimonies from people about their experience of being born again into the family of God. There was a special music presentation and then a moment of silence as the live broadcast from Essen came in.

And then, there was Billy Graham on the screen. He preached the powerful message of the cross that night. The wonderful words of forgiveness and restoration through the cross went deep into the heart of this lawyer, and when the night was over he was standing at the front, giving his heart to this man, Jesus!

What an honor to have worked alongside Billy Graham in bringing the gospel to Europe. We saw 68 people come to the Lord just in our venue in Wiesbaden. Overall, 500,000 people made decisions for Jesus that week!

What was started that year is still going on today with *Pro Christ* meetings every two or three years broadcast from different cities in Germany.

Many a morning have I stood on the porch of my house, and looking northward, have seen the smoke arise from villages that have never heard of Jesus Christ. I have seen, at different times, the smoke of a thousand villages— villages whose people are without Christ, without God, and without hope in the world... The smoke of a thousand villages...
—Robert Moffat

~5~

Medical Missions, Roosters, and Juanita!

We pulled up to the terminal in Managua, Nicaragua. It was so exciting to be in a new country. We would be working with a team from our church and meeting a medical team coming from Georgia. We looked forward to this new adventure.

There was a delay when the plane finally stopped and the door opened for us to deplane. One of the locals on the plane told us that we had flown here with the president of the country, Violeta Barrios Torres de Chamorro. We watched as she walked across the tarmac and into the terminal.

We were able to deplane a few minutes later and head to the area to pick up our luggage. We had several huge boxes of medical supplies and equipment, so it took us a little longer than normal to get through customs. We finally boarded the bus that had been sent for us and drove to a compound that housed a Bible school. Here we would connect with the medical team to do clinics in different villages.

We spread out our sleeping bags and air mattresses, girls in one classroom and guys in another. There was a shower for us, but no hot water. We had brought fans to use (that we left for the Bible school), so once we got accustomed to sleeping on the floor, we made it fine.

We had arrived on a Saturday and had a church service with the minister sponsoring our group that first night. Ken was asked to preach and shared on the blessed hope of the coming of Jesus! It was a wonderful service, with the music always binding us together with the locals.

The next morning, we again boarded the bus and headed for a village up in the mountains. It took us 7 ½ hours to drive there so we were prepared to spend a few nights. On the way, we stopped in one of the cities that had made news in the U.S. just a few weeks before we arrived.

On July 21, 1993, a group of 150 armed men had taken over the city of Esteli by an organization known as the Worker and Peasant Revolutionary Front. The members managed to take over the city for a time. But they had chosen violence to express their views. The conflict lasted two days and 45 people were killed and 98 wounded before order was brought to the city.

When we stopped in this city on August 8th, there were still signs of where the fighting had taken place. The locals pointed out bullet holes in the walls of buildings. Some of our friends in America had thought we shouldn't go to Nicaragua with this recent uprising, but we have found when we're actually in a place, and we know we're in the will of God, there is peace.

We were famished so stopped for lunch here in Esteli. I ordered the two-piece fried chicken meal. I had to get a bite or two of Ken's, though, since my two pieces were a neck and a back, with more bone than meat!

We finally arrived in the village of Santa Isabel, in the mountains of Nicaragua. It had been a beautiful trip, but we were ready to be off the bus. When we drove up, we were instantly surrounded by about 75 children. As we exited the bus, they loved on us and welcomed us as only children can do. Our guide told us we were probably the first Caucasians they had ever seen.

We set up for a church service that first day. The adults had a service and I helped with the kids with a puppet show and stories. Afterwards, the women all fed us a wonderful supper of fried chicken, rice, beans, and tortillas.

Two families completely gave up their homes for the three days we were there. The girls were all in one home, which had a concrete floor. The guys were in a home with a dirt floor. The toilets were outside and the bathing area was a rain barrel in one of the yards with neck-high boards around it for privacy.

The home I stayed in was very basic with just a few tables and chairs around. I didn't see any beds, so they must have taken whatever they slept on with them—probably mats for the floor. Some of their food supply for the winter was piled on the back porch—their entire corn crop for the year. There were chickens in the back yard, along with a cow grazing.

By the end of our stay, I found myself envying these people a little. There seemed to be little stress and they were happy, friendly people. I knew if their corn crop wasn't good and they couldn't feed their families, they had stress and difficulties too, but their simple lifestyles seemed to be much more peaceful than our sometimes frenetic American routine.

We spread our air mattresses on the floor, with our sleeping bags on top. Our group of ladies completely took up the small living room and had just enough room between us to put a few items we might need for the night. When we were all settled, we looked up to see little brown faces staring at us through all the open windows. That became a regular occurrence and we learned to love those little kids!

Our breakfast the next morning was wonderful. They served us fried eggs, beans, and tortillas. I still think of that trip as some of the best food we've had anywhere in the world. Most of our meals consisted of beans and tortillas, but they were homemade on stone ovens by Nicaraguan mamas who knew how to cook. The food always tasted so fresh and good.

The routine for the days was usually a medical clinic during the day and preaching at night. Ken and I would walk around the village during the clinics, trying to connect with people and invite them to the services. The people were so hospitable. They would invite us into their homes and give us the only chairs available. We tried to also just sit on the floor with them, but they wanted to honor us with the chairs. It was very humbling.

On one of our walks through the village, Ken and I came up to the door of a house. A small toddler was there and looked up at us and started screaming and crying! The momma tried to get her quiet, but she would not stop crying. We finally went on down the street to another part of the village, still hearing her cry. We figured out it could have been the big sun glasses and bright pink sun visor I had been wearing!

In the afternoon, it got very hot and humid, and then a storm blew through. It rained so hard, water came into our house and the whole village lost electricity. Instead of outside, that night's meeting was held in a house by kerosene lamp. People still came out for the meeting and found their way to the house.

The next day, after the morning clinic, we all boarded the bus to go to a nearby river. We were just going for a little sightseeing, but all of a sudden the bus filled up with people from the village—children and adults both. They were all singing and laughing. Some of our guys jumped in the river with the kids and played with them. It was an impromptu holiday and was one of the highlights of our trip.

On the last night, we gave gifts to the people of this village. We blessed the families who had given up their homes for us, and also gave the women who had cooked some money for their time spent preparing our meals. But we got a gift in return that surprised and perplexed us.

Early in the mornings of our stay, I mean early—like 3:00 or 4:00 am, one of the roosters would begin to crow. We weren't sure where it was located but found out later it was on the back porch of the house the men had been staying in. On the day of our departure, the host for the guys' house came up to Ken and handed him that rooster with his legs tied. He was giving his rooster to Ken as a gift!

Ken had made the comment after getting awakened too early, "I'm going to get that rooster!" and had been misunderstood. Our host thought he wanted the rooster and was offering it to him. We had quite a time getting out of that and explaining we could not take it on the airplane, but that we appreciated his willingness to give up his rooster.

When we were ready to head back to Managua, our bus would not start. All the men got out in the rain and had to push it uphill out of the parking place and then roll in downhill to start. It didn't start until it was almost at the bottom of the hill, so all the men were wet and covered with mud. We all then walked down the hill in the mud to board the bus. We waved goodbye to our new friends and were on our way.

About half-way back on our journey, the bus broke down. While they worked on it, we got out and walked around to the nearby houses, reaching out to people. Since we were out of the coolness of the mountains, it was getting hotter. After we ate some of the food we had on board, we got some of our mats out to take siestas alongside the road.

We walked to a small *tienda* (store) about a quarter mile away and got cold drinks served in bags. It was almost five hours before another bus showed up. They put us on that bus and hooked the disabled one to it and towed it behind us. We finally limped into our compound around 7:00 pm. We were all so hungry that we opted for a meal before a much needed shower. Afterwards, the shower was ice cold, but it felt so good to finally get our hair washed and feel clean again.

I was sitting on one of the benches of the compound, enjoying the scenes around me and the coolness of the shade. We were taking a day to rest before continuing in other nearby villages. Five of our members had been sick during the night, so we were giving them time to recuperate.

A butterfly of a little girl came up to me with a beautiful smile. She was a little shy, but I encouraged her to come over to me. She was 4 years old and looked up at me with huge brown eyes in a sweet little face. She sat beside me and I was completely taken!

But, no matter how much I talked to her, she never said a word. I began to think maybe she was mute. Ken was soon smitten too by this little creature and anytime we were on the compound, she would run up to us.

We learned from the director that her name was Juanita.

We never saw her with any adults, so just started assuming she was an orphan. Ken and I even began to talk about how we could adopt Juanita and wondered what the process would be like.

In the meantime, anytime I was with Juanita, I would encourage her to talk. We talked to some of the doctors on the team and they didn't think she couldn't speak, but that she just hadn't been shown much attention. She was soon calling me "Bettie" and saying a few other words. The whole team went for ice cream one night and were all delighted to hear her say, "Yum yum" when she took her first bite.

She was wrapped completely around our hearts when we found out a startling discovery—she was not an orphan! Her father was pastor of a church in a village miles away, and was very sick. He and Juanita's mother were on the compound so he could get medical attention in the city. Her mother was busy tending to her husband all day, so they had let Juanita have free run of the enclosed compound.

We went to visit this family and prayed for the daddy of

little Juanita. We still think of her often and she is the only child in any of our travels that we came close to adopting. There was just something special about her!

For all of our outings and ministry trips, a bus had been rented for us by the director. They assigned us a driver to take us anywhere we needed to go, from the ministry trips, to the *pollo* (chicken) fast food places in Managua. He had driven us to Santa Isabel and stayed with us our three days in the mountains. Freddie was available for us anytime we needed him and we soon looked on him as part of our team. I think he felt our love for him and accepted our friendship.

But Freddie joined another team that week. He gave his life to Jesus and became our new brother in the Lord! What a blessing to see this young man become a new creation!

Our week was soon over and we returned home. But the people of Santa Isabel, Freddie, and little Juanita have stayed in our hearts.

*They put fresh heart into the
disciples there, urging them to stand
firm in the faith.*
—Apostle Paul

~6~

A Marketplace Transfixed

We were standing on *Mauritiusplatz* marketplace at an outdoor sausage stand. The cold wind was whipping around us and it was cloudy and gray. This was our favorite place to eat, but it just happened to be an outdoor stand, so we had to eat standing up in the cold.

We had looked forward to this moment for a long time, but we both looked at each other and expressed the same thing. As we gazed out over the marketplace Ken has preached on so many times, it was a strange moment for us.

We had arrived in Germany the day before, and it seemed surreal to us to be standing in the marketplace, eating German sausage and *brochen* (bread). We almost felt a little panic, because it didn't seem familiar and home to us as it always had before, but we soon realized we were experiencing a bit of jet-lag. We also realized we had not set foot in Germany for three and a half years.

As we walked the streets of Wiesbaden and different cities and villages during our two-week stay in the latter part of 1997, our hearts began to beat again with the same passion we've felt so many times before—there is yet a work for us to do, there are multitudes lost without Christ, and there is a message for us to proclaim that can save their souls!

We look back on the years through the mid-90s and know they were growing and maturing times. Some were very difficult and it was hard to know if we were still moving forward in ministry. At times, it seemed just the opposite was true.

At one point we were exploring new ways of ministry and a wonderful opportunity presented itself. Ken was asked to be interim pastor of a church three hours from our house. It was a good experience and we made lifelong friendships.

When this time was up, we had a Bible study in our home and began to draw in unchurched people. As they started to get saved (and baptized), we began to disciple them. This led us to start a church that Ken pastored for three years. It was a unique experience, but after this season, Ken knew he had to get back to his true calling—evangelist.

So in 1997, we arrived in Frankfurt, fatigued from a nine-hour flight and a seven-hour time change. We walked through the maze of customs and immigrations, and looked up to see our familiar old friend Jean-Pierre wheeling toward us with a baggage cart and a welcoming smile. It was a wonderful sight!

It was a great thrill for me to go to a church Ken had been a part of in Mainz, called Der Fels (The Rock). This was the first German church Ken ever attended on his first week on the mission field back in 1984. He had talked about it many times and I felt I knew the pastor and some of the people already. We literally squeezed into their Sunday morning service. At the time, they were moving into a much larger facility and God's hand continues to rest upon this beautiful congregation today.

One of the opportunities we had while on this short trip was preaching in one of Der Fels' house groups. Each Wednesday night, everyone gathers early for a bit of supper. They all bring something, like our *covered dish* dinners here in America.

In Germany, most people eat their big meal at noon, and then have a light supper in the evening. I was amazed at what a "bit" of food there was. We had brought a tray of cheese, grapes, and pretzels. Someone had provided a small can of liverwurst, someone else three boiled eggs and a basket of bread.

I noticed a box of candy on the table, a small block of cheese, a small bowl of cheese dip with more pretzels, a bowl of pistachios, and twelve people waiting to eat! When I looked at the things that were collecting on the table, I thought, "We will never get full on this meal!"

But as we sat around fellowshipping and eating, the true purpose of our coming together was evident. We weren't there to fill our bellies, but our hearts and our souls. When that happened, we were full enough, and the food was delicious.

As Ken began to preach the message of the glorious cross of Jesus to the small group gathered, I could sense the presence of the Lord ministering to their hearts. We had sat in on the house group the Wednesday before and knew firsthand some of the needs and struggles they were having.

Ken felt that more than anything, they needed to be reminded of the heart of this Kingdom—the love and forgiveness our Savior conferred on us when He gave His life on the cross in our place. Ken and Jean-Pierre closed the meeting several times, but people were reluctant to move or interrupt the Holy Spirit's work. Eventually, everyone left, thoughtfully reflecting on the deep work God was doing and not wanting it to end.

Ken had always wanted to take me to two cities that set across from one another on the Rhine River. We took the train to Bingen and then a ferry across the river to Rudesheim.

Rudesheim was especially beautiful! It sat cuddled up against the Rhine River and at the foot of a mountainside covered with vineyards. It was very cold when we visited, but had lots of charm. We would walk down typical narrow German streets with grapevines draped across the top to produce an arbor. There were cozy restaurants and cafés along the streets that invited people in from the cold.

There were flowers everywhere in window boxes. We walked for hours down a tree-lined path along the Rhine, then up the mountainside into the vineyards for a breathtaking view of the city and river. Ken was always eager to share his Germany with me and this town was a special part of our trip as we talked and dreamed of future ministry together.

As we were walking the streets of Rudesheim, Ken was on a quest to find the market square. It was cold and windy and our heads were bent against the wind as we came around a corner. When we looked up, there before us was the marketplace! We both stood still in awe at what was taking place.

First of all, it was on a small hillside, with trees all around, and was surrounded by three-story buildings. It wasn't that large, but a pleasant setting. There was a booth set up in the middle of the square, with festive music playing and lots of people gathered all around drinking warm drinks.

The whole atmosphere was so inviting. It was cold and

windy, but that little booth had provided a cozy, festive place, full of fellowship and warmth, and many had gathered to enjoy it. As we walked away, we couldn't help but talk about how much more the fragrance of Christ could be spread in this same way.

How much more meaningful it would be to have the life-changing message of the gospel coming over those speakers through music and then preaching. To see people drawn into the most glorious of all fellowship—the family of God. The words of the apostle Paul came to mind, "Now he uses us to spread the knowledge of Christ everywhere, like a sweet perfume. Our lives are a Christ-like fragrance rising up to God" (2 Corinthians 2:14b-15a NLT).

As we continued walking and talking that day, we came back to the marketplace an hour or so later so Ken could get a picture of it. As we came around the corner this time, we were again struck by what we saw. There was a marketplace but it was changed completely. The same trees and benches were there, but the people, booth, and music had all disappeared. The atmosphere seemed cold and lifeless.

Three little boys were playing soccer, and the wind was as cold and biting as ever. We couldn't believe the difference and realized how little it had taken earlier to fill this same marketplace with such delightful ambiance and so many people. But more than anything else we realized, that the wonderful message of a Savior and His forgiving love reverberating off those walls could change the eternal destiny of those gathered there.

Our two weeks were soon over and we said good-bye to our friends and boarded the plane for home. But we left with something very important—a fresh desire to pray for open doors to preach the gospel in Germany! We were given hope on this trip that we could walk through these doors and minister once again on German soil. We still had some things to work through, but we were going in the right direction and God was blessing our footsteps.

How sweet is rest after fatigue! How sweet
will Heaven be when our journey is ended.
—George Whitefield

~7~

No Worries, Mon!

We sat in the bus terminal waiting for the bus that would take us to the peninsula of Belize, Central America. The terminal was dusty and meager with wooden boards for seats. There were a few locals sitting around waiting with us. Everything moved slower here and we were already relaxing into this *no worries* atmosphere. The windows were all open and the sounds and smells of Belize City filled our senses. It reminded us of being here eight years ago on our honeymoon. It was a familiar and welcoming sensation.

We had an hour to wait for our bus to Dangriga, where we would change buses for the final leg to Placencia, on the peninsula. While we waited, we pulled out some tuna and crackers from our store of food and had lunch.

There was a commotion outside and we looked out to see a bus pull up. Most of the people inside got up and started to board. Our bus wasn't due for another 30 minutes, but the sign on the front of the bus said Dangriga. We were a little confused but we saw no one to ask for direction, so we decided to board before it pulled away.

We pulled our heavy luggage up the steps of the crowded

bus and found a seat. We were finally on our way to the peninsula of Belize. We had opted for the five-hour *chicken bus* route instead of flying to have the true local experience and to save money.

It had already been quite a day—starting out from Dallas at 3:30 in the morning to catch a "stand-by" flight. We had gone through Miami and flown over the Florida Keys and looked down onto the island of Cuba before spotting the Yucatan peninsula. We had finally landed in Belize City and taken a taxi to the bus terminal. We still had many hours to go before we slept.

During a season of our lives, Ken and I both had to take regular jobs. I worked in an accounting/tax office and Ken went to work in a cargo office at the Dallas/Fort Worth airport. In the midst of some very difficult times in our life, we were provided this brief respite in Belize, one of our favorite places.

Because Ken worked at AMR (American Airlines' parent company), we were able to get tickets on a standby basis, paying only the tax. Since visiting Belize in 1990 on our honeymoon, we had always wanted to return. We were able to get away to this island paradise for a much-needed vacation.

We booked a few days on the peninsula first and then planned to go to the island. We took along camping equipment to camp as much as possible, our own snorkeling equipment, and even a small amount of food.

As we bounced along on our bus to Dangriga, the conductor for the bus came by once we were on our way to collect tickets. When we handed him ours, he told us we were on the wrong bus! We were headed to Belmopan. After the stop there, the bus would then swing back to Dangriga, but it was very much out of our way.

We asked if we did all that, would we still make our bus connection to Placencia. In the Caribbean way, he grinned and said, "Yes…maybe."

A little later, he came back to us and said the bus was going to stop and let us off. We could then wait the 30 minutes for the bus we were supposed to take. We decided to take this offer, since we didn't want to miss our bus to Placencia.

In a little while, we came to a stop, and the conductor let us know this was where we got off. We struggled with all the luggage we had and made our way off the bus. They pointed to a small shelter with a thatch roof and told us to wait there. We looked around and saw nothing but this small shed anywhere around us. No stores, no houses. If the bus did not pick us up, we were on our own!

We were a little uneasy as we waited. We could see the paved road our bus had gone down, but the only other road was a small dirt road that ran beside the shelter. Time seemed to stand still for us, but thankfully the bus pulled up right on time. We again lugged all our suitcases onto the bus, and started down the dirt road we had seen.

It was even more crowded than the other bus and Ken and I had to sit in separate seats. The dust poured in the open bus windows as we clattered along the bumpy dirt road. But we were in the thick of the Belizean culture and it was a wonderful, free feeling. It had been some time since we had been able to take any mission trips, and it felt good to be back in the midst of people, making friends and connecting with them.

We noticed a gentleman sitting in front of Ken, who was also engaging other people in conversation. When his seatmate got off, we could tell he wanted to talk to us. We started to chat with him and he was, of all things, a German who was in Belize on holiday.

As we talked to him, though, he told us something that sent chills up my spine on this hot day, especially knowing we had just sat for 30 minutes out in the middle of nowhere. One of the buses from the exact line we were on was robbed the day before by bandits with machine guns and two people had been killed. We learned later that they had made everyone from the bus lay down in the ditch, and killed two people who didn't cooperate. It was very unsettling as we drove the rest of the way to Dangriga.

In Dangriga, we pulled up to a stop at the bus terminal, and were told we would be there 10 minutes before continuing on to Placencia. I was glad we didn't have to change our luggage to another bus. Ken decided to go inside the terminal and try to call our hotel, to confirm that we would be coming in tonight. We didn't know if our stand-by status would go smoothly all day and get us to the island or if we would get stuck in Miami for the night. So we had left our arrival date open.

I stayed inside the bus to watch over our luggage. Almost as soon as Ken and his German friend stepped inside the building, the driver put it in gear and began backing out.

This was before we had cell phones and I had no way of getting in touch with Ken. I went into near panic mode and ran to the front saying, "You said we would be here 10 minutes. My husband is making a phone call." The driver told me, "We are only going around to the front." I settled back down, hoping Ken would not have trouble finding us when he came back out.

After we had gone to the front, to my utter shock and amazement, the bus took off again! He had just picked up a few people, then off he went again. I ran up the aisle saying, "Hey! Where are you going? Wait a minute!" Everyone was looking at this crazy American. But all that mattered to me was I was all alone on a chicken bus, not even sure where I was headed. Finally, one of the other passengers looked up at me and said, "We are going to Placencia."

The driver seemed to be ignoring me by this time, so I sat back down. I began to plan what I should do and knew the only thing I *could* do was go on to Placencia and hope Ken could get another bus in the morning. I had been up since 3:30 am, was hot, tired, dusty, and had just heard about bandits attacking a bus. But I was on my own for the moment.

When I realized I had no control over what was happening, I tried to relax and pray for Ken that he would also have peace. I couldn't imagine what he would think when he came out and realized I was gone. I knew he would be frantic.

I noticed we weren't really going very fast and were stopping every few minutes to off-load or pick up passengers. After about 15 minutes, I looked up as we slowed to another stop and there was the terminal we had just left! Someone explained that this had become a city bus for the time being. I didn't know whether to get off and look for Ken or stay where I was, but I finally spotted him and his German friend running toward the bus, relief evident on their faces as well.

We were back on the road, headed toward Placencia. Since we hadn't really had time to stop for a meal anywhere, we again went to our small store of food and pulled out cheese whiz and crackers. It was pretty funny trying to squirt the cheese out of the can onto the crackers while bumping along the roads we were on.

We soon had lots of attention as the cheese sometimes landed anywhere but the crackers. We would squirt the cheese, then the bus would hit a bump and the cheese would go flying through the air. The locals around us began to giggle at our predicament and so we started handing out crackers and squirting cheese for them. It was a true ice-breaker and we met some of our fellow travelers that way. It was great fun and a memory!

At one point, we exited the main road and went into a banana plantation. There were rows and rows of bananas and they surrounded us like a forest. When it seemed we had traveled to the center of the banana tree forest, we made a stop and picked up a large group of men—migrant workers on their way home for the night.

The workers were already drinking for the night and were harassing some of the female passengers on the bus. They were getting more and more rowdy and seemed out of control. I was so glad Ken was sitting beside me! I knew Ken would protect me, but I didn't want it to come to that. After an hour or so, they finally exited the bus and we continued on our way south with no further mishaps.

The sun was beginning to go down when our driver pulled over and indicated we were at our stop. We didn't know how close we were to our hotel or if we would have to walk there. We once again stood with our luggage by the side of the road, watching the bus disappear from sight. It was a lonely feeling and we felt a little stranded as the light began to fade around us.

But then we heard someone approaching us. We looked up as a woman came over to us from somewhere in the waning light. She asked who we were looking for and when we told her, she said we were at the right place and to follow her. She was the British woman we had made our reservations with, but since she had not heard from us, she had not been expecting us until the next day.

Oh, what sweet relief as she led us just a few yards to her hotel. We tugged our suitcases over a small bridge and into her lobby. We had finally made it!

After showing us to our room, which was a two-story, thatched-roof cabana with a small balcony looking out over the ocean, she then served us a delicious supper of snook (a delicious white fish), rice, and grilled vegetables. We also drank glass after glass of ice-cold water. It was like a banquet after our eventful day. It didn't take us long that night to fall asleep as the Caribbean ocean waves lapped the shore right outside our room.

We soon adjusted to the laid-back atmosphere around us and began to get the rest we so needed. We spent the next day getting to know our surroundings and visiting the nearby village of Seine Bight. We were directed to a good place to eat and found ourselves on the porch of a small house. The Belizean woman fixed us a wonderful, simple meal of chicken and rice, with homemade tortillas.

One of the things that was recommended for us to do was a Monkey River tour. We made plans to do this and our guide picked us up for the five mile ride down to the town of Placencia on the tip end of the peninsula. There we boarded his motor boat for the 45 minute ride to the mouth of the river. He stopped often and let us take pictures of different things along the way.

We went by a literal tiny one-man island, complete with a shack and outdoor toilet with palm trees swaying in the breeze. We stopped to watch two dolphins playing in the surf. When we came upon mangrove trees growing in spurts along the shoreline, our guide would speed through them, darting back and forth like he was on a race course. We saw many birds and beautiful tropical trees and flowers.

We finally turned into the mouth of the river and rode lazily upstream to a small dock. From here, we walked through the jungle for over an hour. We saw and definitely heard howler monkeys. We stood at the base of a tree full of them while our guide made noises so they would begin their howling. What a distinctive noise!

We also saw many beautiful tropical birds. We were amazed at the giant trees, with their huge roots growing out like buttresses so big we could stand in them. Ken and I both enjoy tropical things, so it was truly an experience of a lifetime.

It was getting warm by this time, so when we got back into the boat, our guide took us to a place in the river we could swim. When he pulled up on the sandbar, we saw a huge mound of sand. He told us these were crocodile eggs. I knew if there were eggs, then there must be a *mama* crocodile somewhere. That made me only put my feet in the very edge of the water, but Ken went out into the deep for a swim. The guide had told him, "No mon, the crocodile won't hurt you, they don't like people," and he believed him!

After a while, though, common sense got the better of him and he also came back to shore. We relaxed a while on the small sandy beach then our guide took us back to the end of the river to Monkey River town. We again had lunch with the locals at a place simply called Alice's.

When we arrived back at our hotel, we spent the evening relaxing in hammocks, looking out over the ocean. We talked about many things, and began believing God that night to make changes in our lives and get us back out to ministry and mission work. God used this restful time to speak to us and put hope in our hearts.

When we first arrived in Placencia, we had also heard about an opportunity that fit in with our plans to camp some on the trip. Gregario, who worked as a guide, came to our hotel and arranged our next stop on our trip. We made plans to spend the next night between the peninsula and Dangriga in the Cockscomb Basin Wildlife Sanctuary, or as the locals called it, the Jaguar Preserve. We made arrangements to get off the bus at Gregario's Mayan village when our time was up on the peninsula.

We told the conductor on the bus where we wanted off, but as we approached what looked to us like a Mayan village, he was not even slowing down. We looked out the window and saw Gregario sitting by his car, so we called to the driver to stop.

It was good to see Gregario's familiar face, and he took over from there. We loaded into the cabin of his small truck and took off up the side of a mountain. It was another bumpy eight-mile journey on a dirt road. We finally came to a clearing with a nice little camping area. We had a thatched-roofed shelter to put our tent under and went to work setting up our campsite. We saw one other couple, besides our guide, the whole time we were in the Preserve.

Gregario took us on a walking tour after we had set up our tent. It was getting pretty hot by now, without the sea breeze to cool things off. But we saw some beautiful tropical flowers and plants—a vine as big as a tree trunk. We saw a huge swath of cleared ground like a highway where leaf-cutter ants had been through. Thankfully, we didn't see any jaguars because they are nocturnal animals. I didn't want to even think about our flimsy little tent!

When we got back to the campsite, we ate more tuna with some applesauce. It was hard to get cool, though, and it was a challenge to get enough of the warm drinking water down to quench my thirst. I opted to stay at the campsite, while Ken and the guide went on the second part of the tour—to a beautiful waterfall where he could swim. It would have been quite a trek just to get there.

I tried to rest some in the tent, but was pretty warm. As I lay there, I heard howler monkeys in the nearby woods. If I hadn't already heard them and knew what they were, it would have sounded more like the growl of jaguars.

When Ken and Gregario returned, Ken told me he had found out that Gregario was a Christian and had invited us for dinner at his house and a church service in the village. We could tell he really didn't want to make the drive back up the bumpy road that night to bring us back to our campsite. He had suggested we *camp* in his gift shop. We were disappointed to not be camping in the Preserve, but with me not feeling very well, we opted to be nearer civilization. So we packed up our tent and went to the village.

Gregario and his family were very hospitable and shared with us from their meager supply. They treated us so special in their small two room, dirt-floor hut. As we were sitting in a hammock-type seat, we looked around and saw chickens outside the open doorway that were completely featherless. We weren't sure what that meant, but they sure didn't look healthy.

His wife cooked us a delicious meal, which included homemade tortillas. When they brought our plates to us we looked down and saw, of course, fried chicken! We silently prayed a little more over our meal than usual.

We were also served orange juice to drink. After we had been eating a while, our host mentioned he had put water in it, with ice. I heard Ken whisper to me, "uh oh!" and realized it was not bottled water.

But I did start to feel better after our meal and we set off with them to the small church. It had been started by missionaries and Gregario's uncle was now the pastor. He asked Ken to greet the people and to say a few words.

After the service, Gregario took us a quarter of a mile up the road to his "gift shop" which was right on the coastal highway we had traveled on by bus. When he had mentioned his gift shop, I had imagined a nice little store with maybe even air conditioning.

But we pulled up to a bamboo hut with no electricity, much less air conditioning. He suggested we keep the front windows closed because of traffic on the highway, and to not keep our flashlights on very long because the lights might attract unwanted attention. As he was leaving, he also locked us in. He was trying to make it clear to us that we weren't in a very safe place! And this is where I was supposed to actually close my eyes and sleep!

When we had set up camp in the Preserve, we realized one of our *K-Mart* air mattresses was defective. Ken blew up the good one for me. He then spread out some small foam pieces we had packed to use as pillows for a little cushion for him on the cement floor.

As soon as we started to try to sleep, a mosquito buzzed my ear. The door and the windows were closed, but since it was a hut, there were plenty of holes for mosquitos to get in. We had also brought a mosquito net, and Ken put it around me, but he was almost carried away by the little buggers during the night. In the early morning hours we figured out the net would go over both of us, but too late for Ken.

We were up pretty early the next morning to catch our bus and were amazed we had slept at all. Gregario came by at 6:00 am to let us out of the hut and to take us back to his house for a breakfast of fryjacks, eggs, and tortillas. We drank more of the orange juice and I had a tepid cup of coffee. We so appreciated this family's hospitality that we didn't want to offend them by not drinking what they so graciously offered us. (We paid for this later, though!)

We said goodbye to this sweet family and waved down the bus going by for Dangriga.

While in Placencia, we had contemplated flying back to Belize City because of the bandits we had heard about. There was a small airport in Placencia that would take us directly to Belize City. This turned out to be beyond our budget and someone told us about a shorter way to Belize City by continuing on the coastal highway from Dangriga. It was dirt all the way, but it seemed a little safer and more direct way to go to Belize City.

But once we arrived at the bus terminal in Dangriga, a man came through the waiting area saying our bus had been cancelled. The only other option was a route going on the Hummingbird Highway through Belmopan. It was also the route the bandits had attacked!

We knew we had little choice at this point, so we boarded the bus. The route had paved roads that were pretty smooth, but there were many stops along the way to pick up and off-load passengers. After a while, we came into an area we hadn't been in before, which was more mountainous and pretty, but even slower as the bus labored up and down hills. I was enjoying the scenery when I realized we had come to a stop in a line of cars and trucks.

I instantly thought of the scenario we had heard about just days before of armed men stopping a bus. I started looking around at the tree line to see if that was why we were stopped. I was so nervous, I was physically shaking. I could tell Ken was concerned too and was checking things out.

We knew these bandits usually stopped vehicles under some pretense and then brought out their weapons. It looked for all the world like this was that kind of development.

As the first anxious minutes passed, we both realized the locals were not responding to this situation with fear, so we relaxed a little. We soon learned the reason for the stop. There was a bridge ahead, over a pretty steep gorge, and it was being repaired. There were men with hammers and nails, hammering what looked like plywood onto the bridge we were getting ready to cross in a bus.

I was still a little worried about bandits. And to think we were going across this bridge in our huge full-sized bus only added to my concern and tied my stomach into an even bigger knot. I really wanted to say, "I'll just walk across, please!" After about 20 minutes of tension, they let traffic cross the bridge and a big truck came across first. I guess he was the test to see if their repair job had worked. We inched forward and finally it was our time to cross. We made it safely across and as we gathered speed, I finally was able to relax.

From there, the road was part paved, part dirt and was

very bumpy again. I was beginning to feel a little sick from all the bumping around and from the scare at the bridge. It was a relief to finally pull into Belmopan. We had five minutes before our bus took us on to Belize City. A woman was selling items to people on the bus and we bought two of her orange juices through the open bus window.

The highway from there was a lot nicer and we only had one more hour to go. When our bus was pulling into the terminal in Belize City, there were taxi drivers already shouting at us, trying to get our business. We had planned to go on to the island that day, so we got one of the taxis and he drove us to the dock.

We had about an hour and a half wait, but it was cool here by the water. We met a local who lived on the island and told us about a good place to stay in San Pedro called Ruby's. She said it was a clean place, but inexpensive. We decided to check it out.

When we had come to the island of Ambergris Caye (meaning *small island*) on our honeymoon, we had flown there from Belize City on a small plane. Now, we were scheduled to get to the island on a boat called *The Thunderbolt*. As we climbed aboard, we saw we were on a 41-foot speed boat with three powerful 250cc engines. We sat close to the back and took off from the pier, well…like a thunderbolt!

We zigzagged across open ocean, going by other smaller islands, but I could hardly enjoy the scenery. I fought to keep my hat and sunglasses on and to keep my contacts from blowing out of my eyes. It was quite a ride!

We knew on leaving that we had not been told any safety instructions and once on board we didn't see any life preservers around. There were cabinets in the back that might have housed them, but there was no way to ask anyone after we took off. After our hour and a half *flight* across the ocean, we arrived safely and with both contacts still in my eyes!

We found Ruby's with no problem, even remembering it from our trip in 1990. It was a very basic hotel with each room having a small bathroom, a fan for cooling, and two twin beds. We could tell it was designed for the backpacking crowd and there were many young people around. We got Ruby's last room but she could only promise us two nights lodging.

As we walked around the island, we realized it had grown since we had been there. It was no longer the sleepy fishing village we had visited before. There were still no huge high-rise resorts, but we walked by a few four and five story buildings that had not been there before. We came across one of these newer structures with scaffolding outside across the balconies. We thought they were still building on it, but realized it was open. We went inside to check it out.

They were doing some repairs, but were still renting the apartments for a much lower price than normal. We looked at one of the apartments and were amazed. It was much nicer than anything we had been in on our trip, with white tile floors, white wicker furniture, and a nice living room and kitchen that looked out onto a balcony. And the price was right!

We made plans to move there when our two nights were up at Ruby's. It was a little loud at Ruby's with all the young people and our open windows. But it was adequate and we spent our days out snorkeling and combing the island on bicycles.

On our second day on the island, the orange juice and coffee Gregario had served us started catching up with us. We had brought Imodium (our *little green pills*) with us and had to take them the rest of the trip. It didn't stop us from enjoying our time, but just a little reminder—don't drink the water!

We moved into the Mayan Princess and were able to eat a few meals in our kitchen. We were also blessed to realize we had air conditioning! I slept the best I had for the whole trip, with that wonderful cool air flowing on us.

We soon found out, however, that even though we were in an upscale apartment, we were still in a developing country. On our second day in the Mayan Princess, the power started going off for periods of time. We were out doing things on the island most of the day, so it didn't bother us that much. When we came in to clean up for dinner, we had water but still no electricity.

When we went out on the street and started toward a hot dog and taco stand, we noticed everyone around us had power, except the Mayan Princess. We knew during the day, the whole island had been without power, so we were a little leery of what we were eating. We were already taking little green pills every day, so didn't want anything else going on.

But why were we the only ones without power? We went back to our hotel and were told since this was the dry season, there was not enough power on the mainland to produce the electricity they needed. So the government had just come out to the island and taken one of the two generators used to produce power for the island.

We heard several stories about all this, one stating that the island was run by the opposing political party to the one in power on the mainland. A little flexing of political muscles, I guess. Because our hotel (and two others on the island) were a little bigger and had air conditioning, the town officials of San Pedro had completely cut our electricity. We realized with some chagrin that we would have been better off at Ruby's, with at least the fans running to get cool.

The owner of our hotel finally worked a deal that he would turn off all the A/C breakers if they would at least turn on the electricity. The rest of our time at the Mayan Princess, we had electricity off and on and even occasional air conditioning.

We made one trip out to the barrier reef, which is about a quarter mile from the island, to go snorkeling. It is beautiful with all the different species like parrot fish, trigger fish, snapper, and even stingrays and barracuda. We saw wondrous sights as we looked beneath the beautiful blue/green waters of the Caribbean.

But we also got a neat surprise just off the pier in front of our hotel. There were also fish all around some rocks the locals had piled there to attract the fish. There was a huge enclosure that housed a giant sea turtle and we could swim right up to it for a good look. You could almost touch the small fish swimming around everywhere, before they would scurry away. It was breathtaking!

On our last night in Belize, we sat on the balcony, looking over the ocean with a full moon shining across the water. Since I was a young girl, that has always been one of my favorite scenes and I was blessed beyond measure to experience it.

We had had many adventures on this trip, but I knew we were going back home refreshed in our minds and especially our spirits. We were ready for how God would lead us in the days ahead—whatever that would be! We didn't know it at the time, but things were getting ready to turn around for us in a wonderful way. God was faithful!

Burn the ships!
—Hernando Cortés

~8~

Carrying the Cross for Jesus

As Ken sought the Lord after returning from Belize, God began to put it on his heart to take a life-sized wooden cross, put it on his shoulder, walk out where people were, and tell them about Jesus.

He had done this before we were ever married. It had all started on a mission trip in Guatemala in 1986. For a three-month period he had served a ministry doing traditional ministry to the people of Central America, with everything from riding horseback to remote villages, to conducting a tent campaign in a large city. During the campaign, hundreds of people had gathered to hear the gospel night after night in the big tent. On the last day, the ministry planned to do a Jesus Parade through the streets of the city. Some people planned to wave brightly colored banners and others to ride horses as they paraded through the streets of Quetzaltenango.

Ken could not figure out what to do in the parade. One of the missionaries he had become close to carried a life-sized wooden cross as part of his ministry. The moment Ken saw the cross, he asked his friend, David, if he could carry it in the parade. To be so publicly and unashamedly identified with the person of Jesus appealed to Ken on a deep level. He not only carried it in the parade that day, but joined his friend on other cross-carrying missions in the States.

This all came back to him as he prayed for a way to do evangelism. In years past, evangelists were invited into churches and held revivals. If you ask most baby-boomers how they were saved, the first sentence usually contains the words, *We were having a revival at our church, and an evangelist was speaking...* But by the 1990s, this was changing.

Churches no longer invited evangelists to speak, so many evangelists just became pastors. Others tried different ways to evangelize. Culturally the lost were also staying away from the churches. And as the gift of evangelist was set aside, churches, of course, became less and less evangelistic. But the true evangelist lives to reach out to the lost!

However it was hard for evangelists to find an audience of unchurched people. As we were praying over the idea of carrying the cross, a woman came up to Ken at church and handed him a check.

This was not that unusual, but when we looked at the check later, we realized God had used her to answer our prayers. The amount was equal to about three months of Ken's salary. We knew with this confirmation, it was time for Ken to quit his job and go back to full-time ministry. We had heard a song that spoke of "burning the ships," and that's what we felt we were doing. The song was inspired by an early part of history that speaks of commitment to a purpose.

In the spring of 1519, the Spanish explorer Cortez landed a tiny army of 600 soldiers on the eastern shores of Mexico. His bold mission was to conquer a land that was larger than Spain. To insure ***total commitment*** from his men he ordered his fleet of ships to be burned! There was no turning back and no other possibility for his crew but to do what they had come to do.

So, Ken burned his ships, quit his job, and began planning how he would do this crosswalk. He decided to carry the cross from our home in north central Texas to the coast, stopping in the towns along the way to witness. He knew from experience that walking the cross down a street was effective—it automatically opened the door for conversation.

He bought a mountain bicycle and a small cart to pull behind it. He made a cross from three pieces of wood that was then put together with bolts. He got a small wheel for the bottom of the cross, so the friction from dragging it wouldn't wear it away. He would ride the bike with the cross and his camping gear and other supplies in the cart and then put the cross together when he entered a town.

It was a Saturday, in the last part of 1999. Rain began to hit our windshield even as we pulled out of the driveway. We were on our way to do a crosswalk just a few miles from our home. Ken had already been to Alvarado the day before and had begun his 300 mile journey to the coast. He had wanted to make those first steps alone, just him and Jesus.

This was the second day and he had planned to walk from Alvarado to another small town close by called Venus. It wasn't supposed to rain until tonight. But there it was, the closer we came to Alvarado, the harder the rain fell.

Once Ken had settled all this in his heart, he went forward with determination and a sense of purpose. This kind of *giving all for Jesus* seemed to come much more naturally to him than to me. He was slightly concerned my parents would think their daughter had married a crazy person, but he still went forward to do God's will in reaching out to people. He would be made a spectacle for Christ, but only for Him!

But this was all totally new to me. I was completely behind him and felt it was the perfect direction for our lives, but I wasn't prepared for the foolishness that swept over me as he prepared to leave. We had pulled up in a convenience store parking lot and Ken was pulling the cross pieces out of the car and assembling it.

The rain was pretty steady by now and I almost wanted to duck my head as I sat in the car. I wanted to tell Ken that we should just go home... since it was raining. And then I remembered a past experience.

We were in Mexico and had traveled to the small village of Santa Rosa with a team from our church. The trip had been one of the most harrowing of my life, with our van traveling over mountain cliff roads barely wide enough for the van. When our team arrived at the village, we had almost immediately turned around to go back down the mountain because our team leaders did not want to make the return trip after dark. Ken particularly felt we should have ministered to the people, even if it meant giving up our comforts and spending the night.

I had never felt such a sense of failure, to have possibly risked our lives to bring the gospel to these people, then to turn around and go home. If Ken and I were ever in a sticky situation all these years later, our cry to each other was "Remember Santa Rosa!"

That cry was coming up in my heart this rainy, bleak morning. I did not want to repeat that situation and just go back home. I knew I had to push through this and get behind my husband. I prayed for boldness and courage for Ken (and me).

In a few minutes, he was ready to start his walk. I have seen my husband in many situations that have made me proud to be his wife, but I have never been as proud of him as that day. He hefted the cross to his shoulder and started walking with those quick, determined steps of his down Highway 67 toward Venus.

As he made his way to the coast, we could see there were many times when he needed someone to be with him and help. I longed to be by his side. While he was close by home on the weekends, I was able to do that for a short time. I drove on ahead in my car and secured him a place to stay at night.

He was encouraged when I drove back to him in the middle of the day with lunch. Later, when he arrived, he and I took the cross together down the streets of that town. What a time of freedom that was for me. There's nothing quite like being a *fool for Christ*.

Ken says the first step is sometimes hard to take, but by the second step, the joy of the Lord is there and it's easy from then on. There is an unbelievable release that comes when you are 100 percent free from what others think about you—when you know you are completely sold out to Jesus.

And there's also the reward of looking into someone's eyes who is comprehending (maybe for the first time) the concept of a loving Savior – to see a life being touched before your very eyes – right out there on a busy city street. The more I walked beside Ken with the cross, the more I was hooked!

In that short time with Ken, I found my place again beside my husband. I remembered one of my wedding vows, *I will go with you.* I wanted so much to be with him in ministry.

After he completed the walk to Galveston, Ken then went from our home northward, to the border of Oklahoma. We called this 500 mile journey from the border of Oklahoma to the coast *A-Cross Texas.*

He talked to many, many people but one of the most meaningful conversations of the whole trip happened at the end of his journey to the coast. He was walking the cross through the streets of Galveston. As he walked down a back street in a poor neighborhood, he saw a young man sitting on his front porch. He had his feet up on the banister, just staring into nowhere.

As Ken passed only a few feet in front of him on the sidewalk, pulling the beautiful life-size wooden cross, his eyes got big and he leaned forward and asked incredulously, "Why are you dragging that cross through here?" Ken explained that he was trying to get people to think about Jesus and the tremendous sacrifice He made to save us from sin.

The young man looked at Ken soberly and said, "Mister, that's all I've been thinking about lately."

They began to talk and had a wonderful time together. He was so open with Ken and told him he had only gotten out of prison recently and desperately wanted to change his life. At one point he confessed to Ken that he had been a crack dealer most of his life and that he didn't want to keep living that way—"going in and out of jail," as he put it.

He was utterly astounded as Ken opened up his Bible and had the young man read aloud—"If any man is in Christ, he is a new creature. Old things pass away and all things become new."

He abruptly got up without a word and marched into his house. Ken wasn't sure what was going on, but he came back with a pen and paper to write those life-changing words down right then and there. He was practically beside himself as the truth of this scripture touched his heart. He said, "I've never seen anything like that in all my life."

Ken prayed with him, and then encouraged him in his new faith. They both knew God had sent Ken to him at this exact moment...at the end of a walk across Texas.

He talked to people from all walks of life, from homeless in Jasper to lawyers in Jacksonville. He had been invited inside beauty parlors and beer warehouses to talk to people. Newspapers had written articles about him, which gave him the opportunity to preach the gospel to entire towns as he gave the interviews. It was the trip of a lifetime and brought to memory something that had been in his heart for years for Germany.

Ken had always dreamed of going from border to border in Germany, witnessing for Jesus all along the way. Germany is such a small country (about half the size of Texas), so we knew what he had done in Texas could be done there. We began to pray and make plans for Ken to walk the cross in this land that was always on his heart.

Blessed be God, I have broken the ice!
—George Whitefield

~9~
Von Füssen nach Flensburg!

Our journey to this place and time in our lives really began many, many years ago. As a young missionary in Germany, Ken was full of zeal and anticipation of what God would do in his life. He had come to witness on the streets of Germany with an organization called Teen Challenge. Every missionary is part-explorer, and as Ken traversed and discovered the city and eventually the country, he soon realized where the people of Germany congregated.

In every city, there are streets blocked off just for pedestrian traffic called *Fußgänger Zonen* or foot-goer-zones (FGZ). In the middle of these there is always a market square, sometimes even several throughout the city. When Ken worked with Teen Challenge, they held outreaches on these squares, preaching to those milling about. There were always hundreds, even thousands walking by—some eager to stop and listen.

A dream was born in his heart in those early years, to go from the bottom of Germany to the top and talk to people about Jesus on as many market squares as possible. There was a town at the south tip of the country called Füssen and one at the north tip called Flensburg. *Von Füssen nach Flensburg!*

(From Füssen to Flensburg!) became the cry of his heart and he prayed for the time this would be a reality.

So in the summer of 2000, that prayer was answered in a way he could never have guessed or imagined. The dream had been rekindled during his walk across Texas, so we would now take the life-sized wooden cross Ken carried here in the States and go from the bottom to the top of Germany!

I was working at the time, so didn't think I would be able to join Ken. At first, Ken planned to walk the whole length of Germany with the cross. I was going to take my vacation and join him for a couple of weeks in the summer. As I talked to one of the women who faithfully prays for this ministry, she was a little surprised that I wasn't going with Ken.

She pulled out her Bible and said she had read something recently and felt it was for us: "Two are better than one, because they have a good return for their labor: If either of them falls down, one can help the other up. But pity anyone who falls and has no one to help them up." (Ecclesiastes 4:9-10 NIV).

Something in my heart told me this was right—that she had found the mind of the Lord as she prayed for us and searched the scriptures. Ken and I had always felt we should be together in ministry, but we had made ourselves willing to sacrifice this if needed for him to be able to return to itinerant evangelism ministry.

But God was letting us know loud and clear, it was He who wanted us together. It took several months for the details to work out, but I also quit my job and we took the second step in "burning our ships."

A short time after that, the thought came to us to rent a car. I could drive ahead, secure the hotels, and pick Ken up at night if necessary. We immediately went to the Internet and typed in "car rental" for Germany. The only site that came up was "RV rentals."

We looked at each other and felt just like in the cartoons, a little "idea" light had popped up over our heads. As we pursued the idea, it became so clear how perfect it was. The rental per day on the RV would be about the same as a car rental and a motel each night, and we would have a place to cook our own meals and relax at night.

We began to prepare earnestly for this mission. We were in contact with friends in Germany who helped us find a good deal on the RV rental. Our friends even promised to loan us pots, pans, towels, and sheets for the journey. To transport the cross, we found a ski bag that was the perfect luggage. The cross comes apart into three separate pieces, and they are connected with bolts, so the three pieces fit nicely in the ski bag. Since this was pre-9/11, we had no trouble getting it on the airplane. We got a few strange looks when we told airline agents what was in the bag, but never had any problems.

Together, we boarded the plane in mid-June and wouldn't return until Labor Day.

Once we arrived in Germany we realized the narrow roads with nothing but ditches on each side would never work with cross-walking in mind. It would simply be too dangerous for Ken and for people trying to swerve around him. We changed our plans and decided to drive between the cities instead of walking all the way. We also only had the RV for a month and knew that didn't give Ken time to walk 600 miles. We purchased a bike and our friends loaned us a small trailer and another bike. We would camp as close to the market squares as possible, then ride bikes with the trailer carrying the cross to the center of each city.

As Ken and I climbed into our "rig" to leave, we were apprehensive. We had no experience whatsoever with driving or operating a motorhome. Could we really take this huge vehicle through the narrow streets and roads we had seen? Even though our RV was only 18 feet long, it seemed gigantic for this miniature country.

It was just as scary as we thought—getting used to driving an RV on strange roads. Ken had not driven much in Germany since the public transportation system there is so excellent. We were, therefore, not familiar with the different road signs. The only sign similar to ours was the stop sign; the rest we had to figure out.

One sign we learned pretty quick was the blue and white campground sign. It was always a beautiful sight to see and we sometimes found it just in time before making a wrong turn. We had a book with all the campgrounds listed, but the directions usually told us the major road and then just said *the rest of the way would be marked.* They always were, but sometimes we had to weave all through the city before finally spotting that beautiful sign!

We had picked up the RV just south of Frankfurt. As we looked at the map and planned our route to Füssen, we had decided to take the straightest route, over what looked like scenic roads. After all, that's the way we would want to travel in America, get off the freeways and see the countryside. We were about to see how wrong this thinking was.

As we wound through small village after small village, we realized we would never make any time. Plus, at each curve in the villages we held our breath and hoped nothing scraped the sides as we drove past centuries-old buildings protruding out over the very, very narrow streets.

Sometimes we would see a truck coming toward us and wonder how we would ever pass without hitting. At times one of us literally had to drive on the sidewalk to get past. Even though this is quite normal in Europe, it made for some very nervous moments.

After only going 30 miles in one hour, we started looking for the nearest autobahn. The Germans invented the highway system of on-ramps and exit ramps and they work to precision in Germany. No one ever passes in the right-hand lane; slower cars stay to the right as they were intended to do. That leaves room for the stretches of highway that have no speed limit and cars whisk by at over 100 miles an hour. In our RV we were only supposed to go about 60 mph, so we kept out of the left lane as much as possible.

We got to the autobahn and found our travel much easier. We had a nice wide highway with plenty of rest stops for gas and food. It took us eight hours to drive to the bottom of Germany. When we got close to Füssen, the autobahn ended and we were again on "scenic" roads. Just before we got to our campground, the road actually wound through the middle of farm yards, like someone's driveway.

We pulled into a campground beside a lake, just at the foot of the Alps. It was beautiful! The bathrooms, shower areas, and dishwashing areas were 5-star amenities and the nicest we would stay at the whole trip. It was the closest thing to our starting point—Füssen, and even here we would have a three mile bike trip each way.

We settled in for the night and soon got our routine down with our travel—putting down our jacks, hooking up our electricity, and putting our awning out. Our bed folded up over the driver and passenger seats during travel and had to be pulled down at night. We soon learned the way other campers did things and adopted their routines.

We had never operated a RV before, and didn't realize how different their system is to ours here in the States. And to further complicate matters, our instructions had all been in German, with a strong Bavarian accent (which made it hard for Ken to completely understand).

Most people showered in the bathrooms and washed their dishes in the sinks provided for that purpose by the campground. Unlike here in the States where we hook up to water with a hose and hook up another hose that empties the potty, we learned that any fresh water we used in the RV was going to have to be hauled there in a container (by Ken) and hauled away in another container (also by Ken) to a dump site. Sometimes this was all near the RV and other times it was quite a distance, so we learned to conserve and use the facilities as much as possible.

We realized the dishwashing ritual was something most of the German couples did together and soon we were walking with the procession with dish towels over our shoulders, carrying our dish pan full of dirty dishes. Ken also joined the potty-emptying brigade each morning. Our potty was an enclosed container underneath the bathroom. Ken would pull it from an outside compartment and carry it to a place just for emptying. It was all quite tidy and worked to "German" meticulousness.

Füssen

The day we had waited for all these years finally arrived. Ken would start in Füssen, walking the cross, witnessing to people on the market squares, and go all the way to Flensburg.

Before we left the campground, we both spent time alone—praying and preparing our hearts for this day. We both felt such trepidation, not knowing how the German people would react. I had been reading Acts a great deal (for courage) and verses about suffering kept popping up to my attention. We had no idea what awaited us this day, but we wanted so much to be obedient. I knew Ken was out walking by the lake somewhere, fighting the same "inner" battle I was.

As the time approached for us to leave, Ken popped his head in the door and said, "I just read 2 Timothy 1:8 where Paul says, 'Don't be ashamed, then, of witnessing for our Lord; neither be ashamed of me, his prisoner. Instead, take your part in suffering for the Good News, as God gives you the strength for it'" (Good News for Modern Man Version). That phrase touched me the same way it had Ken. It gave us courage to go out and face whatever awaited us.

We completed our preparations for the three-mile bike ride into Füssen. Ken had a small trailer attached to his bike with the cross latched on with gummy bands. I had a blue plastic beach bag filled with literature, water, the camera, and of course, raincoats!

This would be one of the few days during our trip that the sun shone brightly all day. It was a beautiful ride, at the bottom of those majestic Alps, and as became our pattern, we rode single-file along the bike path that Germany provides in every city. Even in this somewhat rural setting, the paths were as nice as the road beside us. Only in the middle of cities did we ever have to ride with the cars.

When we arrived in Füssen, we went directly to the middle of the city. We found a small park where Ken could assemble the cross. He then went out looking for the market square. We were right next to it, with the entrance to the area through a small tunnel between two buildings.

Ken took the cross underneath a tree and I could tell he was, for once, as nervous as I was. At one point I went back to our bikes for something and my knees were shaking as I waited at the traffic light. When I got back to Ken and saw those three pieces of wood become the cross, I knew we were committed. Words to the song by Stephen Curtis Chapman went through my mind: *My heart is racing and my knees are weak as I walk to the edge…So sink or swim, I'm diving in!*

I'm still not sure why, but as it came time for us to go, Ken sent me ahead through the tunnel to take pictures. Maybe he just wanted to make the first step alone or he could see how nervous I was. He told me later, he knelt down by the cross, asked Jesus for His help, then stood and put the cross on his shoulder and started walking. Before he even got through the tunnel, only a few yards away, he had already stopped to talk to someone. I was waiting on the other side, wondering…

But in a few minutes, he burst through the tunnel, in that quick, bouncy step of his and with a grin on his face. I knew then that everything was going to be fine. Ken had made the first step of obedience and then Jesus had taken over. I don't think any other crosswalk will ever be as hard to begin as that one was. But God was so faithful!

One thing Ken had thought might happen was that the Germans would simply ignore us. But just the opposite was true. People immediately began stopping Ken, wanting to know what he was doing. This was the question he always waited for, because it gave him the opportunity to tell them about Jesus.

As Ken walked down the picturesque narrow street, I stopped to take a picture. I looked over my left shoulder and a man had stepped out of a very exclusive dress shop and was watching Ken go down the street. I turned to go hand him a tract and he blew kisses to us with both hands. I was thrilled when I came closer to learn that he spoke English. He told me that he was Aramaic and that yes, he did believe in Jesus. He was overjoyed with what we were doing and invited us to come into his shop for refreshments.

We talked to a steady stream of people that day and gave each person some literature. The German people were proving to be open to Jesus!

At the end of our day, we wound back around to the dress shop owner and he served us orange juice as his affluent clients looked on. He told Ken he was bringing light to Germany, and as he walked he was spreading that light. This day was my first encounter on the streets with the people of Germany and I'll never forget his kindness and encouragement.

We put the cross back on our bikes and headed to our campground. It was an exhilarating ride as we praised God for the way He had helped us. There is nothing that can compare to the happiness of overcoming the fear of man and being obedient to God.

George Whitefield is a favorite 18th Century hero of ours.

He was a part of the Church of England, a very conventional and staid church. When he first broke out of the church format and preached open-air, he exclaimed, "Blessed be God, I have broken the ice!" We felt the same—that we had broken through the barriers that had kept us from the market places of Germany all these years.

The next day was Sunday, and after a worship service together in our camper, we decided to be tourists, since we were so close to the famous Neuschwanstein Castle. It is one of Germany's most famous landmarks and is the castle Disney recreated for Disney World.

We were anticipating a quiet, leisurely day, but had no idea what a grueling day we had ahead. We took the bus to the small village of Hohenschwangau, just past Füssen. This was the birthplace of the famous king, and the place to buy the tickets to see his home. We were shocked when we arrived to see thousands of tourists milling about the shops and streets. We heard more English here than German.

When we finally got to the front of the line, we found out the next "English" tour would not be until much later that day. We had three hours to kill, plus now we would miss our bus back to the campground. We felt committed at this point and plunged on ahead with our "relaxing" day.

We ate a small lunch at one of the outdoor stands of bratwurst and fries and then headed up the side of the mountain. It was a 30-minute walk and we soon learned why people were paying even more to ride one of the buses to the entrance of the castle. It was quite a hike and one of the hottest days we had experienced in Germany. We found a slightly shaded spot on the castle steps to wait our turn to go in.

Finally the time came and we wound through the small

area open to the public. We were able to see the huge church-like hall that was the throne room and King Ludwig's personal apartment. In his bedroom, everything was very elaborate, fitting a king's taste, including a fountain in the form of a silver-plated swan.

There were breathtaking views from the windows that were open to the mountains and valleys around us and we could see why he had chosen to build here. I tried to imagine what it was like as his home—looking out over the beautiful mountains and countryside. How peaceful it must have been. But it was not to be a place of peace for him.

King Ludwig II of Bavaria started building it in 1869, and was still in the process of building after 17 years. It has never been completed and never will be to keep it historically accurate. Once a few rooms were finished, enough for the king to move in, he only lived in it for 172 days.

He was quite eccentric, especially in areas like castle building, and was even known as the Fairy Tale King. He began to pile up huge debts and seemed to be headed toward spending the entire fortune his family had amassed over 800 years. The government, including his family members, decided to declare him insane. He was finally declared to have mental illness by physicians who had never examined him.

He was arrested and taken to a castle that had been converted into a prison for the monarch. He and one of the doctors assigned to him were taking a walk one evening through the castle park. When they had not returned by 7:00 PM, a search party was formed and the two were found dead in the lake.

It was never known if they were murdered or committed suicide. A cousin of King Ludwig was convinced it was an escape attempt that failed. Whatever happened, it was a sad end to the king many considered to be mad, but was probably just in the wrong profession. He had an aversion for war and liked to spend his energies (and money) on operas and magnificent artwork and buildings. Because of his eccentrics, Germany now can boast several beautifully preserved castles.

As we started back down the mountainside, we chose a path that was supposed to be a little shorter. It was, but we soon realized why—it had an even steeper grade. After almost running down the side of the mountain, we made our way back to the bus that would only take us as far as Füssen. We would have to walk the three miles from there back to our campground.

On the way into Füssen, we had seen a sign indicating there was a McDonald's there. Many places are closed on Sunday, but we knew that would be open. That sounded so good to us so we started asking the locals how to get to it. It was always "just around the corner," and by the time we finally found it, we had walked over a mile.

After we ate, we then had to walk back that mile and then head for home. We finally arrived at our campsite around 8:45 pm. We had walked about ten miles, which made it a very long day, but we were able to see one of Germany's most beautiful areas. Now on to business!

Schongau

We started out the following day for our next camping site in Augsburg. The rain had arrived the night before, and we hardly had a day without rain the rest of our journey. On the way, we were headed for the town of Marktoberdorf, north of Füssen, to do a short cross walk. We were about halfway there when we came to a detour that took us miles around.

We were still on the way to Augsburg, but were nowhere near Marketoberdorf. We decided to stop in Schongau instead. It was really tedious getting into the city, with narrow, hilly roads. (We were still in the foothills of the Alps.) Ken pulled into a parking place at the end of a row of cars parked on the street. We found the machine to purchase our parking ticket, and hoped and prayed it was OK to park an RV there.

We found the market square and realized because it was so small there were not that many shops; which also meant there were hardly any people around. We found a Turkish kabob shop and stopped for lunch. As we ate outside on the small table provided, the young Turkish man came out to smoke and talk. He suddenly began to pour out his heart to Ken and we could tell he was lonely.

He had moved to Germany with his family several years ago and they had opened a shop in another city. He had recently branched out on his own to Schongau and had not made many friends. I could tell Ken was telling him about Jesus, and that He would be a friend to him. He listened to what Ken had to say. Ken asked me to go back to the RV and get one of our books for him as he continued to talk. We went away feeling that maybe he was the reason for our detour to Schongau.

Augsburg

The campground in Augsburg was very pleasant with plenty of trees, and even had a lake nearby. The lake had a path that wound all around it, with benches for resting. Several of the campgrounds we stopped at were beside German lakes and were set up like our state parks. The campground attendant told us we could park anywhere we wanted. This didn't happen very often—most told us exactly where to park. Ken picked out a corner place with a little grove of trees behind us.

We thought we had the "perfect" spot until about 10:30 pm when we realized we were right by the dumpsters. German beer comes in glass bottles and Germans drink a lot of it! In Germany, they have huge dumpsters for each type of glass—brown glass, white glass, and green glass. Each of these dumpsters has a small opening in the top, so you have to drop the glass bottles in one at a time and is engineered for the glass to break. We were kept awake when someone decided to get rid of all their bottles at 10:30 at night, even though most of the campgrounds had a 10:00 "silence" rule.

We found out we were about 3 to 4 miles from the center of Augsburg and even in this remote area, we had a bike path to the city. We were going to ride into town the next day (July 4th), but woke up to a downpour. We learned quickly that this doesn't keep people off the market places, but it does hamper giving out literature and getting them to stop and talk. As the day and rain wore on, we decided not to do a cross walk that day. Ken rode on into the city to check things out and I headed to the laundry room.

We were up early the next day, getting ready to go into Augsburg. It took us about 45 minutes to ride into the city, with a stop at a bakery. These are very common in Germany and they have all kinds of little cakes and breads on display in their windows. The German cakes are not as sweet as ours and make a nice breakfast. Even the smallest village has a bakery and serves up warm, flaky goodies every morning. We couldn't resist as we rode by on our bikes. We took our apple streusel outside to the table and chair and relaxed a few moments before going on.

We rode to the beginning of the pedestrian zone, where

others had parked their bikes in the numerous bike racks. The only place we could see to put the cross together was beside the street where people were crossing at an intersection. Many people stared and gawked at us as Ken put the cross together. When he stood up to begin walking, as happened so many times, a young man wanted to talk immediately. Ken talked to him about 30 minutes with others walking up and listening in. One man who walked up was a Christian and just wanted to encourage Ken.

We found in Germany that people were much more honest than here in America. They were more honest about their relationship with God and would proclaim clearly if they did not believe in God. We could work with this honesty much better than someone who just mouths the words, "Yes, I'm a Christian. I always have been," or "I walked the aisle of a church years ago."

This could be discouraging when the German people flatly refused to accept our tracts, but we found that they also didn't take them and then throw them away once they had walked off. We only found one tract ripped up and thrown away the whole time we were in Germany. That doesn't mean it didn't happen, but it seemed if we could get them to take the tract, we felt they would read it.

We were on the main square of the city, when the black clouds that had been hovering over us finally let loose with raindrops. We learned early in Germany that people do not go home when it rains, they just head for the nearest awning or shelter until it quits. We did the same and stood with others waiting for the shower to pass. It was there we met Harold. Ken talked to him the whole time it was raining and we found a very lonely, single man. He knew what he wanted in a family and knew these times and ages were not very conducive to developing that kind of family.

His heart was reaching out to us and to something more for his life. He listened intently to Ken as he shared the Gospel with him, and he promised to read the book we gave him. He told us, as the rain slowed to a drizzle then quit, that there were lots of people waiting for Ken to come talk to them. They might be afraid to approach him, but they wanted someone to give them answers. We felt encouraged and grateful for the rain that had placed us in contact with this seeking soul.

We went back to the main square and I sat on a bench as Ken walked around the square. A lady came up to me and even though she spoke no English and I spoke very little German, I could tell she wanted to know what we were doing. I had our digital camera in my lap, so I began to show her the pictures I had been taking that day, and pointing to words in the tract in my hand. I knew I was only getting the basics across, so when I saw Ken close by, I motioned for him to come over.

Sybil was a country woman from Bavaria and I could tell by her appearance and demeanor was not very confident of herself. That might have been why she approached me while Ken was not there. Ken was not aware of this and as he came to talk, he sat down on the pavement at this gentle woman's feet. I thought how perfect it was that Ken humbled himself before this woman and honored her in this way.

He then began to share the Gospel with her. She was Roman Catholic and said she did not know she could have a personal relationship with God. Ken explained that she could and invited her to pray with him. She told Ken she couldn't pray with everyone looking on, but she might pray when she got home. Sybil is one that I hold close in my heart as I remember back on those we came in contact with.

As we checked out of our campground the next day, we

came across the German reasoning that often leaves us baffled at the lack of common sense. If it is written on paper, then that becomes law in people's mind. When we checked in, Ken had written the wrong date for our departure on the paper he filled out. Even though the woman in front of us knew we had only stayed three nights, the paper SAID four nights.

This German logic that we have found in many situations will not easily let go to basic understanding, and we had a few minutes of convincing her we were leaving right then and not tomorrow. Finally she saw the mistake she was making and our exchange ended friendly, which we were very grateful for.

Stuttgart

The ride to Stuttgart that morning was one of our worst driving days of the whole trip. The stretch of autobahn we were on proved to be a heavy-traffic area and between Augsburg and Stuttgart there was even a mountain we had to go down. There was a terrible traffic jam and we inched along as we wound down the steep grade. When we finally arrived near Stuttgart, we didn't know which exit would be best to get to our campground, and we chose a street that wound all through the middle of the city.

The city sits in a valley, so we again had to wind our way down a grade—this time on city streets. We felt we were still going in the direction of the campground, but our blue and white signs had seemed to disappear. Since there are very few parking lots in the middle of cities, we were always a bit terrified to think about turning our "rig" around. So we anxiously tried to never make any mistakes with our turns.

We were desperately looking for the next sign, and thinking we might have missed it, when we entered a tunnel underneath another street. As we popped out the other side, we both saw the sign pointing the way. Ken maneuvered into the right lane to make the turn and we followed the signs to the campground entrance. We were so relieved to finally be off the busy highway and sitting at our destination!

We realized from our camping manual (and experience) that all the campgrounds took two to three hours off for lunch—they would close for that time and lock the gates! We had arrived during their lunch break, so we had a while to sit just outside the gate and get our breath. When we finally pulled into the camp, we realized it was not very pretty at all. There were not many trees and we would be parking on cement. But we were thankful that it was so close to the middle of the city and wouldn't be that far to ride our bikes. There was even a subway station nearby if we needed to get into the city by train.

Ken went on into the city that afternoon to check things out. I was pretty stressed out after our ride and felt like all the changes I'd experienced in the previous few weeks were just catching up with me. I felt completely drained, and the last thing on my mind was trying to minister to people. I just didn't feel I could do it.

When Ken arrived back at the campsite, he was completely overwhelmed. It was the biggest city we had been in yet and there were literally tens of thousands of people on the streets. In one of the market squares, they were holding some kind of festival with rows and rows of booths with all sorts of food and wine for sale. It reminded him of Vanity Fair in the book *Pilgrim's Progress*—complete sensory overload. He told me he didn't feel he was ready to do a crosswalk the next day, so we decided to spend the day seeking the Lord and praying.

For me, that night was the low point of our whole trip. I

had been a little sick for days from diarrhea and just wanted to be home. I had taken our trip serious from the beginning, but that night it became clear to me that we were in a fight—light over darkness. As we sat in our camper, Ken began to talk about his trip to the coast of Texas at the beginning of the year and how he had been tired and down one night in his hotel room.

As he prayed, a song came to his mind and he was so encouraged by it. There in our camper, he began to say the words to the song—just as the singer had done as he quoted Isaiah 40:31: "They that wait upon the Lord shall renew their strength. They shall mount up with wings as eagles. They shall run and not be weary. They shall walk and not faint." The words were a balm to my soul and as we listened to music and bits of sermons that night, we began to feel encouraged.

There was a beautiful park between where we were camped and the middle of the city. Ken realized we were very near where he had lived for a short time in 1987. He remembered the park and had spent hours walking around in it and praying years ago.

We rode our bikes there the next morning and spread out a blanket for the day. Ken went for a walk and left me there to pray and read the Bible. What a wonderful thing it is to take the Word of God in our hands and read it and be encouraged. I received strength and encouragement as I sat overlooking ponds with ducks and geese.

As Ken found his way back to me, it was starting to rain. We hadn't bought any groceries lately, so decided to try to find one of the grocery stores Ken used to go to. By the time we found it, it was pouring rain. Ken had the trailer on the bike, so we took boxes from the store and made a cart out of our trailer. We rode the mile back to our campsite in the rain and found all our sheets and blankets (that I had left to "sun" that morning) completely soaked.

We woke the next morning to a cold, rainy day. The *USA Today* indicated that the rain would end in the morning and then be sunny. We were learning the hard way that neither the *USA Today* nor the German newspapers had a clue what the weather would be like. We had rain all morning and finally decided to go on into the city in the early afternoon. By the time we arrived, the rain had slackened enough for us to press on.

As we put the cross together in a park, several people came up to talk to Ken. He even had two kids who must have thought he was putting together some sort of ride. They ran over and sat on it. We took pictures of them and laughed as they sat there looking up at us. It really helped to relieve some of the tension I had been feeling about this walk.

As soon as we walked onto the FGZ, people instantly surrounded us. I didn't see how we were going to even move. It would be like trying to walk through a mall at Christmas time, carrying a life-sized cross. Ken reached down to take the nail from the foot of the cross so we wouldn't gouge someone as we walked by them. I soon learned that if I walked around the wheel, it helped Ken not to mow people down as he walked.

We had gone about 10 feet when of group of young teenage girls stopped us. Sophie (who was named after Shophie Scholl, the brave young girl who defied the Nazis and was killed) did most of the talking for the group and was so interested in what we were doing. She had blue hair (before this was a common thing to do) and was very energetic and outgoing. She seemed to want to be just like her namesake—fearless and brave!

She asked Ken at one point if he was a Lutheran or Catholic, and Ken replied that he was just a simple follower of Jesus. She smiled and said, "Oh, so you're a non-conformist." She seemed to identify with someone who would pull a life-sized cross down a busy street.

One of her friends asked Ken if she could have the nail he was carrying in his hand. As he pressed it into her hand and told her she could, he reminded her of the nail prints in Jesus' hands—to always think about that when she looked at this nail.

We walked all up and down the pedestrian streets, talking to people. One of the incidents that stands out in my mind was toward the end, when we were on a market square. It was getting late in the day and the square was almost empty. In fact, we were heading back toward our bikes when two young men came up to talk to Ken.

One of them was particularly interested in the cross and Ken talked to him for about 30 minutes. Alex seemed so eager to hear the Gospel and seemed to take in all Ken was telling him like a baby bird gulping food.

While Ken was still talking to Alex, another young man walked up and waited till they finished then engaged him in conversation. He was a Muslim and was one of the most knowledgeable that Ken has spoken with. He was not the least bit argumentative and just seemed to want to talk about spiritual things. He gave Ken complete liberty to express his views, as Ken did him. After an hour talking with him, we parted ways and again started heading back to our bikes.

We had a long walk to go, and it never failed that's when we had some of our most meaningful talks—when we were not really trying to engage people in conversation. We were pretty hungry and tired by this time, but sure enough, we had one of the most precious talks of the day. A middle age woman and her little boy stopped us. At first, Ken said she was very agitated and could not figure out why we were identifying with the church. As Ken began to talk to her and revealing the person of Jesus, she softened before our eyes.

She told Ken as a child she had been very curious about Jesus, but had been told by the church and adults to keep quiet. They discouraged her questions and made her feel they were not important. Ken was able to put one of our books, *Who Do You Say That I Am?* into her hands and told her he had written this book just for her. It was a book about Jesus—who He was and what He said—that we had had translated and printed in German. By the end of the conversation, her whole countenance had changed and she assured Ken she would read the book.

We finally made it back to our bikes and took the cross apart. We went to a nearby McDonalds to eat and then rode the 30 minutes back to our camper. On the way back, we passed a circus and decided to come back for it. It was a small tent circus and was one of the most entertaining we have ever been to. Just one ring and we were all close enough to see everything. They didn't specialize in a lot of glitter and extravagant costumes like our circuses here in the States, but were more artistic, funny, and entertaining.

Heilbronn

Our next stop was to a campsite near Neckarsulm. It was as close as we could get to our next stop, Heilbronn, which we were told was about 2 ½ miles away. It was a beautiful campsite, and as I look back, my favorite. We were directly below small mountainsides, covered with vineyards. In the evenings, we took walks through these vineyards. We were also close enough to the small village of Neckarsulm to do some much needed grocery shopping.

When we got back to the campsite, Ken decided to scope out Heilbronn for the crosswalk the next day. He took off on his bicycle and I washed out some laundry by hand and wrote postcards. When we had first arrived in Germany, we had bought two inexpensive cell phones. A couple of hours later, Ken called to tell me he still had not made it to the center of Heilbronn and his bike pedal had just broken. He estimated he had ridden 4 or 5 miles so far. There was nothing for him to do but push the bike home, but he wanted me to know it could be hours before he arrived. He figured out how to ride with one pedal, so he made it back faster than he thought.

When things like this happen, we have to remind ourselves that we have put our footsteps in the Lord's hands. We think back on people we talked to in specific cities, and realize OUR timing was not always the Lord's. Often, when we felt hindered and behind schedule, invariably we had some of our most significant, divine appointments. If it hadn't rained all morning in Stuttgart, we would never have met Sophie or the middle-aged woman who desperately wanted to know about Jesus.

So as we walked through the beautiful vineyards that night, we gave this new predicament to God and tried to relax and get things in perspective. As it turned out, the next morning Ken was able to fix the pedal well enough to continue.

The next day was a very difficult day for Ken. I had decided to stay at the campsite and let him ride into Heilbronn by himself. All the "attention" we were getting carrying the cross was beginning to get to me and I felt I needed some private time on my own.

When Ken called me around noon, his day had not been going well at all. He was not engaging anyone in conversation, but he decided to stay and keep trying until at least 2:00 pm. Right after he talked to me, a small group of teenage girls came up and wanted the tracts he was offering. They caused a crowd to come to see what was going on and when he looked up he had about 40 kids around him.

As he was talking, a German Christian came up and started talking to the kids too. He obviously knew the teenagers and was telling them what Ken was saying was the truth. Ken went on to have several great talks with people after that.

Heidelberg

The next day we made our way to Heidelberg. For once, it wasn't raining that morning, so we made good time. The camping ground was a small strip of land right beside the Neckar River. When we backed into our space, our back window was only about 12 feet from the river. We could sit at our kitchen table and watch everything from huge barges to swan families going up and down the river.

The rain was even unusual for Germans. This was July and it had not only rained almost every day, but the temps were in the 40s some days, with a whistling wind. It seemed to be getting colder too as we made our way from the south to the north of Germany. When we had first rented the RV and were shown how the heater worked, we had no idea how often we would need it now in the middle of summer. We finally had to buy winter coats for our bike rides into the city centers.

It rained for two days solid. We tried to get some of our errands done during this time. Instead of our bikes, we caught the bus into town. Since we had no TV in the motor home, it was very hard to know what the weather was going to do. We walked to the main train station to purchase a *USA Today*. We also needed to find an American Express office to cash some of our traveler's checks. And we looked for an internet café. We finally found one on a little side street and were able to communicate with our families and the people handling our finances back home.

The next day looked a little more promising. It was cloudy, windy, and cold, but no rain. We finally set off for the city center on our bikes with the cross. It took us 30 minutes to get there, and we were discouraged as a brief shower passed over us. We were both quiet on this ride, praying and thinking about the day to come.

Somewhere around Stuttgart, I had decided I was not as comfortable with thousands of people staring at me as Ken was. Also, if he was engaged in conversation, others would come to me, expecting me to talk to them in German. That made me very uncomfortable if they could not speak English. We finally worked out a plan that from now on I would hang back, away from the melee, taking pictures and praying. This worked well, and gave me the liberty to join him when I felt comfortable.

Heidelberg's FGZ is very long and narrow, not like some that go out from the center like a spoke. We parked our bikes at one end and put the cross together to walk the length of the FGZ. Even before Ken got the cross put together, he had someone engaged in conversation. After this man walked away, another shower was over us, so we stood huddled together under an umbrella trying to keep our literature dry.

Since Heidelberg is a university city, we talked to people from all over the world. We talked to young girls from China and Japan. Later, a young Asian man broke off from his group of peers as they began to scoff and make fun of Ken and the cross. Ken talked to him for a long time. When he finally rejoined his group, we could tell they were teasing and mocking him for talking to Ken. But he had been so hungry for Jesus' words of eternal life that he had not cared.

As we came to the other end of the FGZ, we stopped at a McDonalds to eat. Ken "parked" the cross out front, so we could keep an eye on it through the window. Right as we sat down to eat, a very heavy shower poured down. We not only were staying dry, but the cross was under the awning out front and not getting wet either.

As we walked back down the long FGZ to our bikes, the crowd had thinned considerably because of the rain. We were always on the lookout for that last person to talk to and sure enough, we found him. Two couples stopped Ken and were arguing with him about the validity of the Bible.

As Ken began explaining the evidence and historical facts that are available for supporting the Bible, three of them moved away, leaving one young man alone to listen. The other three kept trying to get him to move on with them, but he refused. At the end of their conversation, Ken put a book in his hands and he promised he would read it.

Another talk Ken had as we approached the end of the day was with an older man who started drilling Ken with questions. Ken answered him with simple, honest answers. Then all of a sudden, he opened his heart to Ken and told him he had once gone to Africa as a missionary. But he had seen so much petty infighting amongst the churches and denominations that it had practically shipwrecked his faith.

He said that even though he was a theologian, he had no use for the church. In fact, he scarcely believed in the church at all. Then he told Ken he believed in what he was doing and thought it was the only hope to reach these everyday people on the streets because they have no regard for the church.

By that time, he had practically reached a crescendo emotionally. He suddenly took the New Testament Ken was holding and looked at Ken earnestly and straight into his eyes and said, "This is the only thing that really matters—you are doing it. Just keep doing what this says." He took one of our books, handed the New Testament back to Ken and walked off into the crowd.

Even as Ken took the cross apart, a whole Romanian family came up and wanted to talk. They had come to Germany on vacation and we were there another 45 minutes, ministering to this family.

We finally rode back to our motor home at 7:00 pm. About the time we arrived, a huge, violent thunderstorm broke over us. It lasted about 30 minutes and would have drenched us if we had still been on our way home. We thanked God for our timing that day with the rain showers and for all the people we had been able to talk to.

Kassal

When we mapped out our trip from Füssen to Flensburg, we decided to skip Frankfurt and the central area of Germany and come back to that on our way back down. As we made our way ever northward, Ken decided we would go on toward Flensburg, and then use our remaining time to visit cities along the way back to the RV rental company. Since we had only rented the RV for a certain amount of time, we could better gauge our time that way.

We next headed for the city of Kassal. Our campsite was about 2 miles from the main part of town, with a beautiful park to ride our bikes through on the way. It was one of the most beautiful parks I had ever been in, with breathtaking ponds and lanes of trees. It truly felt like heaven, especially with a little sun popping out from time to time.

But the next day, it was back to cloudy and colder weather—51 degrees. I guess people were speaking optimistically, because all we heard the day before was the weather was getting better. Because of the previous nice day, we were a little shocked and discouraged to have showers on us again. We finally just gritted our teeth, and left on our bikes for the city center.

As we arrived, a shower of rain came. We huddled in a corner under the umbrella with the cross still on the trailer. We both had been struggling that morning, but as we looked at each other, we grinned and decided to make the best of this day.

Our first stop, after only walking a few feet, was to talk to a punker named Bastion. He had a Mohawk haircut and spiked dog collar around his neck, but he was very meek and friendly. He truthfully told Ken he had not thought about Jesus much. He wasn't rude or mocking and listened to what Ken had to say, and then took one of our books.

We talked to many people on the market square, but there always seemed to be one person who touched my heart. We had walked with the cross to a group of street people. Ken tried to give them tracts, but they only wanted to argue, so we moved along.

But there was one man sitting away from the rest. His hand was obviously recently bandaged and he was sitting with his head down, like he had lost all hope. When Ken passed out the tracts to the other street people, he had been missed. Right as we started toward him with a tract, he was on his way to us to get one.

After we had walked away from him and were down the street, I looked back and saw that he was reading the tract.

Flensburg

We spent one night in Hannover and then drove all the way to Flensburg the next day. As we rode through Hamburg, we had to actually go through a tunnel under the Hamburg harbor. It was two miles long and was a little claustrophobic, especially since we had had many *Staus* (traffic jams) that day. (*Staus* in Germany seem to be much worse than here in the States. Maybe there are not as many options like frontage roads like we have, but sometimes people sit and wait for hours. People just get out of their cars, walk around, and have a coffee from their thermos.)

My mind was running a little wild with the thought of billions of gallons of water not that far above our heads. We had also heard of an accident not long before we were there where a car had caught on fire in the tunnel and sucked the oxygen out, killing even more people. As we started through, I found myself almost holding my breath that we would not get stopped. I was so glad to finally pop out the other side.

At last we came to the northern tip of Germany— Flensburg! You could actually see Denmark from the harbor. We were in a campground about 3 miles from the city center. As soon as we got set up, we took off on our bikes to Flensburg to check things out.

As we rode along, we could tell it was getting cloudy and even heard thunder, but by this time in our journey, we just had to keep going in the rain. If we waited for clouds to clear, we would never get started. Since the day had dawned so warm, we had left windows open in our motor home.

When we arrived, Ken went to the Tourist Information Office, that is in most German cities, to buy a map. We locked up our bikes and then walked across the street to a market place. Almost as soon as we stepped onto the square, it started sprinkling on us. We went into one of the shops and when we came out it was raining even harder.

We stood under an awning for a while, waiting for the shower to move on, but the rain just kept getting harder. We finally went inside another one of the shops like the other Germans were doing, since the awning was no longer keeping us dry.

As we all huddled inside, the storm intensified even more, and then we saw something that Ken said he'd never seen in Germany—it started hailing, with strong winds. We were safe and dry, but I started thinking about the motor home, with all the windows open.

When it finally subsided, the streets were running with water and as we looked up one street, the police had it blocked off. We headed toward the harbor to see what it looked like, but the street closest to the harbor was completely flooded. Cars were still driving slowly through and people were walking through the flooded waters, carrying their shoes.

I had wanted to find some seafood to eat beside the harbor, but the restaurants we were headed to were flooded. So we ate at Pizza Hut that night. When we arrived back at the motor home, we were shocked (and praising God!) that no water had gotten in with all that wind and rain.

The next day, we headed for Flensburg with the cross. We had noticed the further north we got, the less approachable people were. We had a hard time getting people to talk to us and they didn't want to receive our tracts. Ken even asked me to stand with him, thinking he would be more approachable that way, but that didn't work either.

We walked up and down the FGZ and along the harbor, with very few contacts. As we rounded the corner where we had left our bikes, there was a big group of young people gathered having their picture taken as a group. As we approached, they gathered around Ken and were very interested in what he was doing. There were two chaperones with them, but they didn't seem to mind the kids talking to us.

Ken started speaking German to them, but they looked confused. He heard one of them speak, and realized they were from England. They were in a trampoline club from Manchester. We didn't have any English literature with us, so Ken told them his testimony and preached to them about Jesus. I don't know that I've ever seen such attentive, eager listeners.

As Ken came to a close with what he had to say, a hush fell on the group of young people. One girl pointed to the cross and said, "I do believe." Another seemed to take courage and chimed in, "Me too, I believe." Ken had not given a formal invitation, but they were responding out of their hearts. It made our less-than-stellar-day end gloriously!

Kiel

As we made our way back down through other German cities, our first stop was another harbor city called Kiel. As we drove, I always had a lap full of maps and campground information. I was reading the description for the one we had chosen out loud to Ken. "It says the way into the campground is *eng und steil.*" Ken said, "I know *eng* means narrow, but I'm not sure about *steil*. I grabbed my vocabulary book. "Oh no! it means steep!"

We had been on some pretty harrowing roads with this rented motor home, and couldn't imagine how bad it was if they had to warn us of the drive in. We were almost there, though and decided to go ahead and try it. It wasn't even as bad as some of the other roads, and we breathed a sigh of relief.

Once we got settled, we found that the main part of Kiel was on the other side of the harbor, but buses came right to our campground. We had never travelled on a bus with the cross though, and looked for other ways over to the city center. We found a ferry system that would take us across, along with our bikes and trailer.

We had bought a paper and it indicated the day would be sunny. But as it happened so many times, the next day was rained out! Ken used the day to walk in some woods nearby to pray and seek the Lord, and I did laundry and cleaned our little home on wheels.

We got out early the next morning to ride the mile on our bikes to the harbor town of Möltenort. From there we would catch the boat to cross the harbor. We didn't know if there would be a problem with the trailer carrying three large pieces of wood hooked to Ken's bike, but we paid for our bikes to ride with no question. We were headed for Kiel with the cross!

As we went down the FGZ, we talked to several people. They were a little friendlier than Flensburg. We talked to people from Norway and a man from Trinidad. One older man who had lost an arm in the war was very upset with us because we were Americans. He was shouting at Ken that Americans had taken his arm and would not talk to us. So Kiel turned out to be a mixed bag.

Toward the end of our day, we came across a man from New Zealand who was a Christian. He and his wife seemed desperate for Christian fellowship and invited us to come to their house for dinner that night. We decided to take our bikes and the cross back to the campground, and then come back across the harbor to meet them. They would drive us back to our motor home after we ate.

As the boat docked in Möltenort, our day ended like most had in the last month—rain. By the time we got the bikes and cross to the motor home, we were drenched. We changed clothes and waited for the downpour to end. By that time, we were running late on catching the boat back, so we rode our bikes instead of walking. That meant our new friend would have to drop us at the boat dock in Möltenort instead of bringing us all the way to the campground.

They fed us a wonderful dinner, and then soaked up our encouragement like starved people. We were finding it hard to leave them, and started trying to get the ball rolling that way about 9:30 pm. But they simply did not want us to go and since they were driving us home, we stayed until 11:30 pm.

It was almost midnight when we arrived in Möltenort where our bikes were parked. I hadn't quite anticipated this mile-long midnight ride back to our motor home. We had ridden our bikes all through Germany, but none of the rides stand out in our minds like this one. The wind was blowing, with no stars or moon. There were a few street lamps along the path, but some of the way was dark and eerie.

During the day we had enjoyed this path right by the water, but now it seemed precarious. We finally came to the *narrow and steep* road into our campground. There was a car with a group of youths parked at the entrance, obviously drinking and carousing, but we glided on by without incident. I was never so glad to arrive back at our safe little motor home.

Bingen

As we drove the next day, headed south, we had to once again go through the tunnel in Hamburg. I try not to "worry about tomorrow" but I have to admit I had been dreading this tunnel the whole time we had been up north. We were listening to the radio to see if there were any traffic jams in Hamburg.

We heard there was one in the opposite lane, but ours was clear. We even noticed there were traffic lights going into the tunnel to stop people from going in if there was congestion. Our light was green, so we sailed on in, with the Hamburg harbor over our heads.

I was pretty nervous, looking over at the other lane not moving. Our lane slowed a time or two, but we never had to completely stop. It was so good to see daylight ahead and finally pop out the other side.

We arrived at our next campground in the town of Rüdesheim, next to the Rhine River. We wanted to go across to Bingen for the crosswalk, so road our bikes with the cross onto yet another ferry.

We got the cross put together and started down the small FGZ. As we stood in one of the market places, a couple who were both blind came by with their sighted 3 year-old. The man almost tripped over the cross and Ken reached out to keep him from falling. Ken then invited him to feel the cross to understand what we were doing.

As we stood there talking, the little girl ran off to play on a toy in the square. I could see how precarious this was as the mother began to call for her to come back. Being a child, she was totally disregarding her mother. Ken explained to her what her little girl was doing and that she was fine. It gave us a few moments to talk to this couple.

We walked along the FGZ to the end, talking with different people along the way. We were resting by a fountain with a lady sitting across from us with her small son. Ken tried to get a conversation started, but she ignored him. Finally as we were about to move along, she asked Ken what he was doing.

As Ken began to explain, she became very antagonistic and angry. She erupted and said she didn't believe in a God who would let wars and famine happen. She was like so many other Europeans we've encountered. As we try to talk to them, we hear an explosion of emotion as their only reference for Christians is the Crusades or the Inquisition carried out centuries ago. They also lash out about their misconception of God as the one causing children to starve or the evil in this world.

As Ken had done so often before, he let her have her say and then began to tell her about Jesus. He told her what God was really like instead of the version she had heard about. Ken told her that God had sent Jesus into this sin-filled world to be its Savior.

I was standing alongside, but couldn't understand most of their conversation. I could however, see the change in her countenance. Even her voice changed and I could tell she was receiving the good news about Jesus. Ken talked to her over an hour and she took our book about Jesus with almost reverence. She promised she would read it and when she left us she was smiling and wishing us well over and over.

Ludwigshafen and Mannheim

Our time in the motor home came to end, but we still had weeks left on our trip. There were many cities in the center of Germany we had skipped on our way to Flensburg that we still intended to visit. We were staying with a friend just south of Frankfurt, so we rented a car and headed for the cities of Ludwigshafen and Mannheim, just across the Rhine River from each other.

We stopped first in Ludwigshafen and walked the cross. We then headed toward the river after a while and found the bridge walk to cross over to the Mannheim side. It was a little unnerving to cross that mighty river on foot and look down and see the swirls and currents moving fast below us. Once across, we encountered people all along the way as we reached Mannheim and headed for the FGZ.

We walked about three blocks and then came to the first market square on the FGZ. There was a huge fountain in the middle of it, with seats all around. There just happened to be a camera crew setting up for shots of the square. Some of the crew came over to Ken to see what was going on. This helped to attract attention for us and Ken soon had a crowd of around 25 people around him.

Ken had "parked" by the fountain, and that's as far as we got in Mannheim that day. It was the shortest cross walk of the whole trip. Where we normally walk for blocks and blocks, we only walked a few feet and stopped. The camera crew had helped set his table and he stood there the rest of the afternoon, talking to different people. We grabbed something to eat at a nearby Pizza Hut and then headed back across the river to our car.

Worms

The next day we headed to the historic city of Worms. We parked our car on the street and then walked to a nearby small square beside a Catholic Church to put it together. We noticed a gate and Ken read a plaque telling us this was the gate that Martin Luther had escaped through during his trial in that city.

As we walked down the narrow FGZ, we came to a street called Jewish Street with a small square called Synagogue Platz. We went inside the Synagogue and found out we were in the oldest synagogue in Germany. It was originally built in 1034, but was burned to the ground during *Kristallnacht* (Crystal Night) by the Nazis. It was rebuilt in 1961 (using some of the original stones) and still serves the Jewish community.

We continued our walk and a woman with a beautiful smile approached us. We had noticed a couple of boys playing and she said her oldest son (8 years old) was interested in Jesus and always had been. She said he felt a kinship with Jesus and asked if Ken would talk to him. Oh yes!

As we continued, three little girls started talking to us and walking alongside us. We try to be especially careful with our interactions with young ones like this, so were not encouraging them much, but they persisted. We finally walked with them to a playground where there were lots of kids, some even teenagers. There were many people around, so we talked to the kids and gave the older ones books.

As we started back toward our car, we were again stopped by kids, from about 8 to 12 years old. More kids kept coming to see what was going on and they listened intently to Ken explain about Jesus. We usually never have the opportunity to talk to children, but we began to realize that today had been "Kid's Day."

As we finally made our way to our car, we were filled with such joy. We felt so free and were waving and smiling at people as they drove by gawking at us. It was a moment of pure joy in having done the Father's will that day!

We took the cross apart and headed back into the center to eat. We had noticed the FGZ was very small for this city. As we walked we found the main part of the FGZ that we had totally missed! It even had a Martin Luther Square. But we also knew we had been right where we needed to be that day—for Kid's Day.

Wiesbaden and Frankfurt

After a crosswalk in Wiesbaden, where Ken had lived as a missionary in the 80s, we decided to go by train the next day to nearby Frankfurt. Since it would be pretty heavy for Ken to carry the ski bag with the cross, we divided the pieces and started walking up the street toward the train station. We realized later we should have just put the cross together, but instead he had two of the pieces and I carried one. People were staring at us even more than usual. We found the joy in it though as we tried to look casual carrying our wood down the street.

When we got to the train station and boarded, Ken put the cross pieces up on a luggage rack and we were off. Now the cross had been on planes, boats, and trains!

Our reaction in Frankfurt was tepid at first; we think because they see so much here in this huge city. We finally walked on to the famous Römerberg Square. We were able to have good conversations with people there and give out many of our books.

Mallorca, Spain

We had spent two months on the road and had planned a small vacation. As with any excursion like this, we pay for this out of our personal account, and so we knew we could not spend much. We had thought about a trip to nearby France or Czech Republic, but as we sat in the travel agent's office, we came across what they called a *Last Minute Deal*. It did truly seem like a deal, so we booked a trip to Mallorca, Spain. Just like anything else, you get what you pay for and we had no idea what we were in for.

Our first clue was the check-in time for our flight—4:20 am! We arrived on the island of Mallorca about 7:00 in the morning with very little sleep. We were herded into a group where we sat to wait for the "transfer" bus. We were literally a herd of people who were all being dropped off at different locations throughout Palma, the major city. We had no idea what our hotel was like and was hoping it would be better than some we were seeing as people got off the bus.

When we were finally dropped off, the girl at reception told us our rooms wouldn't be ready until 1:00 pm. We had hours to wait, and were sleepy and hot. We went out to the beach to wait. We picked out a nice cabana by the beach and two lounge chairs. There were not very many people out and about, so we were soon nodding off.

We went back early to our hotel to see if we could get into the room. She had one available by then so we checked in. It was such a disappointment—more like a cabin than a nice hotel. And no air conditioning! It was only 9:30 in the morning and already stifling in our small room.

We went back to the beach, to the chairs we had picked out earlier. The beach was filling up and our day was not getting any better. About that time a man came by wanting money for our beach chairs that we had "rented" all morning without even knowing it. Another huge disappointment that I had not considered was the sunbathing habits of most Europeans. Let's just say they're not nearly as modest as we Americans are!

Our dinner and breakfast was included in our room. We had assigned tables and we were to share our meals each time with two young East German men. We thought how perfect this was and tried over and over again to engage them in conversation. They were not interested in talking to Americans, so our meals became awkward times for Ken and me to talk to each other.

We were running on two hours of sleep the night before, so everything seemed extremely negative that first day. We tried to go to sleep about 9:30 pm but had to have our patio doors open for any breeze. We were in a cluster of hotels and by a busy street, so it was very noisy outside. There was also very little privacy, since there were hotels just across the street from us.

Then someone a few patios from us (we think our table buddies) cranked up a loud jam box that went on until about 11:00 pm. We had six more nights booked, but I was ready to get the first flight back to Germany the next morning! So much for this *deal!*

But, thankfully, God's mercies are truly new every morning. We actually slept very well, got through our breakfast, and then headed out to the beach. We tried to find a spot away from the throng of people next to the water, and found some palm trees at the edge of the beach next to the sidewalk.

It was much quieter here and we didn't have to shell out more money for our shade. We found a McDonalds for lunch and then set off for the nearest hardware store. We found a small electric fan for about $25 (worth every penny!). We were able to shut our curtains against the afternoon sun and still have air moving. It was a wonderful improvement!

That evening after dinner, we joined the rest of the people and walked along the promenade as the sun set. This became our regular routine and one thing we missed when we left. It was so pleasant to walk among the locals and feel part of their community.

We rented a car one day and drove to the quieter end of the island, to a harbor town. We love walking among boats at a harbor. We also found huge cliffs with water breaking on rocks below us. It was very peaceful and quiet, much more to our liking than the jam-packed Palma area.

We even found a small beach in a cove on the way back that had mostly families and kids swimming. It seemed like Paradise as we swam, with the beautiful aqua water splashing against boulders on each side of the cove.

The travel at the end of our trip was just as inconvenient as flying to Mallorca had been. We had to check out of our hotel by 11:00 am and didn't fly back to Germany until 11:00 pm! It was an experience that we can add to our memories' file, but for relaxation we both much prefer quiet places with solitude in mind rather than noisy throngs of people. Ever since this experience, whenever we're in Germany now, we still see signs in travel windows that say *Last Minute Deals,* but we just walk on by!

Munich

We arrived back at our friend's house where we were staying in-between travel. He had to go to Munich, so we decided to go along for one more crosswalk in this great city. The FGZ was crammed with people and we spent most of the day talking with different people. But the crowning moment came when Ken was able to explain the gospel to an older man named Horst, who said he was an astrophysicist.

The first thing he said to Ken was, "My young man, my recommendation for you is that you take this cross of yours, break it into pieces, and throw it into the garbage can—with your faith." He went on, "Do you understand physics? Have you ever studied astrophysics? Are you well-educated?"

Then he boldly said that science had long since proven there is no God and that because of science *he* had all the answers to mankind's needs. He told Ken, "Evolution is a proven scientific fact and there is no God!" He refused to take our book or talk about Jesus.

When Ken was finally able to speak, he told Horst that he was a man of love and really didn't want to argue. But if Horst wanted to have a friendly discussion, then they could certainly talk about some of these things. When Horst agreed, he didn't realize that Ken had studied much on these very subjects.

They spoke for more than an hour and by the end Horst was speechless and flustered. Ken had rather easily demolished his great belief in the "fact" of evolution. Ken proved that evolution is one huge balloon full of hot air used to intimidate believers in God and creation. But with only a little truth, it can be burst and quickly deflates, and can be seen for the utter foolishness it is.

At the end of their talk, Horst humbly accepted our book about Jesus.

Our two and a half month journey all over Germany was coming to a close. We said our goodbyes, then flew to London and then on to Dallas Fort Worth. We had just spent a very cold summer, and even the few days of sunshine we had had in August were not that warm and already over. We were certainly not prepared for the 111 degrees on Labor Day we encountered when we deplaned at DFW. And to cap off the irony, Texas had not had any rain in over two months. What a difference from our almost daily cold rain showers. But it was good to be home and to sleep in our own bed.

We talked to many, many people on the streets and market places of Germany that summer. We were interviewed by a newspaper, invited into homes where we spoke with people until almost midnight on several occasions— sometimes encouraging believers, other times helping a lost person understand saving faith in Christ.

We preached in churches, to youth groups, and did a "Fishers of Men" seminar open-air. The cross was transported by plane, train, ship, bike, and by foot, and was seen by tens of thousands of people. From one end of Germany to the other, we watched hard, cold, unbelieving faces change before our very eyes into joyful, friendly, warm ones as we simply talked about the person of Jesus of Nazareth. It was the trip of a life-time and we were so grateful for the opportunity.

"Not called!" did you say? "Not heard the call," I think you should say. Put your ear down to the Bible, and hear him bid you go and pull sinners out of the fire of sin. Put your ear down to the burdened, agonized heart of humanity, and listen to its pitiful wail for help. Go stand by the gates of hell, and hear the damned entreat you to go to their father's house and bid their brothers and sisters, and servants and masters not to come there. And then look Christ in the face, whose mercy you have professed to obey, and tell him whether you will join heart and soul and body and circumstances in the march to publish his mercy to the world.
—William Booth

~10~
Land of the Swinging Hammocks

It was a normal evening for us as we sat watching our local evening news. But, then they began to share *Breaking News* and we watched in horror as they reported on the devastation happening in El Salvador. It was February, 2001 and an earthquake had struck that land and almost a thousand people were killed instantly and hundreds of thousands of homes destroyed or made unlivable.

As the days went by, another quake struck and killed over 300 more people and caused more people to be homeless. The cameras showed us pictures of the tragedies and one in particular struck Ken's heart—the image of a little girl standing under a tarp. This was her family's new home.

As we continued to watch different news stories of the tragedy, Ken was silently praying, *Lord, send people to help them.* It was one of those times when he knew he heard the Lord's voice speak into his heart, **You** *go help them.* The scripture came to him, "Anyone who wants to serve me must follow me, because my servants must be where I am" (John 12:26a NLT). He shared with me what he wanted to do and then began to plan his trip to this ravaged country.

We could see from our news that the damage was extensive. Since Ken wasn't even sure there would be hotel rooms available, he put together equipment and prepared to camp while there. Because of these unknown factors, we decided it would be best if he went without me.

So just a few days after the second quake, Ken was on an airplane headed to El Salvador for a week of ministry. Besides the camping equipment, he also had his life-sized wooden cross.

When he arrived, he was able to hire a young man to serve as both driver and translator. Erick was invaluable to him and seemed to know just what Ken's mission was and how best to help him fulfill it.

One of the first things Erick advised him was to not camp out. There were some hotels that had not been damaged and it was much too dangerous for an American to be out by himself. There was the great danger of abduction of foreigners, especially in this unstable time.

So Ken took his advice and checked into the Holiday Inn. He and Erick went out each day, to different cities affected by the quakes. He saw camps full of people living in squalid conditions. These camps where people had fled from their unstable (or destroyed) homes were a haphazard collection of ragged tents and dwellings thrown together with tarps, cardboard, and a little bit of tin.

It had been several weeks since the first quake, but Ken saw no other aid workers about. He was told they had already been there and left. But there was still much work to be done. (There was another major earthquake in India 13 days after the El Salvador quake and the world's attention and resources had quickly shifted to this region. We later heard that the ministry *Samaritan's Purse* went to El Salvador a little later and built many, many houses.)

But in the meantime, there was so much suffering all around it was overwhelming. On the first day, Ken put the cross together and then he and Erick went to one of the camps to offer spiritual help and to pray with people.

He walked up to the first dwelling of cardboard and plastic tarps. An older woman sat in front with a couple of small children. Ken, through Erick translating for him, began to tell her that she was not alone and that Jesus was with her. He spoke to her about ten minutes and then prayed for her.

Her reaction was friendly and cordial, but no joy registered on her sad face. These people had lost everything—their homes, their possessions, their livelihood, as well as hundreds of loved ones and neighbors in the space of about 40 seconds. Now they were living under tarps with no hope of anything better. Ken said he felt his words to her that she had not been forgotten seemed hollow and resonated back to him in mockery. He said he felt he'd been hit in the head with a 2x4, utterly overwhelmed!

Instead of plunging forward to the next group of tents, he stepped back about 20 feet to think and pray. As he did this, Erick lingered a little longer, speaking to the people in Spanish. When he came back over to Ken, Ken told him, "We have to go to the market and get something for these people." Erick then told Ken that was exactly what he had been discussing with the people, asking them what they needed most. He told Ken they asked for powdered milk and food.

They immediately left the cross where it was and went to a market. They filled Erick's trunk with bags of beans, rice, and powdered milk. They also bought candy for the kids, who desperately needed a little joy in their lives.

They returned to the same camp, and Ken retrieved the cross. Within minutes, the whole camp joyfully surrounded them, this time animated and excited. Ken prayed with them and then the head of each family came by and received a bag of rice, beans and powdered milk.

After this, Ken walked the cross through the camp and talked (and listened) to the people. They wanted to talk about all that had happened to them. One lady told Ken the story of a neighbor who was killed when a wall fell on her.

Others told of hundreds of their friends and loved ones simply disappearing forever under a wave of earth in one of the many mudslides that came after the quake. Sometimes, all Ken could do was hug the people as they cried, and tell them Jesus came to heal their broken hearts. When it was time to go, it was hard for Ken and Erick to leave these people who had so much sorrow. But they had at least given them a little hope and encouragement.

This began the pattern for the rest of the trip. Ken and Erick would fill up his trunk with food, then head to different camps. Ken had not taken that much money with him, but could not go out without taking these desperate people some hope in the form of food. He pulled out his credit card and continued to buy food each day.

He was able to call me a couple of times and explained the situation. By the time Ken got back home, the generous people in our church and our partners in ministry had helped make up the difference and the credit card was paid!

On one day, Ken went to the biggest camp in the city with several thousand people. When he and Erick entered the camp with the cross, a huge group gathered around them. They were totally surrounded, so Ken began to preach to them. They responded so beautifully to the very tangible presence of Jesus. Ken then prayed for them all.

He then began to go up and down the rows of tents, stopping, preaching, and praying for the groups that gathered. Sometimes he stood and preached, and other times he sat down in the midst of the groups, hugged the little children, and encouraged the adults. As Ken explained it, in the midst of all the suffering and hurting, there was a connection with these people that was completely incomparable with anything else he had ever experienced.

I believe it was the compassion and love of Jesus shining through him to the people. They recognized it and responded to it. As Ken and Erick began leaving to go through the gate, the people followed them and didn't want to let them go. They had felt the love and compassion of Jesus!

So far, Ken had visited camps or makeshift tent cities that were thrown together in any open space like a park or soccer stadium. But when they visited the city of Cohutepeque', they found a very different situation. They asked a policeman where the quake victims were located, and were informed they were scattered throughout the city.

The damage to this city was much more severe and was a result of the more recent quake just days before Ken left the U.S. The streets were frenzied and full of milling crowds. They searched about 45 minutes for a place to begin, but nothing seemed to be clear.

Erick was growing more and more uncomfortable and finally told Ken there were serious problems in this city with gangs who kidnapped and robbed people often. He had told Ken there were areas a foreigner would not be safe, and this seemed to be one of them—even without the added turmoil from the earthquake.

As they drove on and on, looking for a safe place to park the car and begin the crosswalk, these words began to affect Ken. A small battle began to rage in his mind. He would be so conspicuous with the life-sized cross on his shoulder. But he also knew the cross was a disarming symbol and could equalize the situation. He felt once they got started, it would be all right.

Erick finally found a place to park and they put the cross together. They strung bags of food over the horizontal beam of the cross and then loaded themselves down with the rest of the food they had bought. They walked for a few blocks, looking for people, and finally found them near the town center. They were simply living in the dusty streets and sidewalks, next to their crumbled homes.

In the organized camps, people had tents or tarps for cover, but here many had no shelter whatsoever. They had just pulled couches or beds from the rubble and were living out in the open. They had a few pots and pans and were trying to live in these conditions. Ken and Erick approached them, one family at a time, and gave them bags of beans, rice, milk, and candy for the kids.

As Ken went from city to city ministering, there were still quakes going on. One day while they were out in one of the outlying cities, they heard that there were more quakes going on in San Salvador. When they returned to the capital city, they could tell people were on edge and learned that five quakes had occurred in 6 minutes, with the worst being a 4.2 on the Richter scale.

He had already experienced small quakes in his hotel room, but that night he was awakened by a strong jolt. He felt the building swaying and heard it popping and groaning. It seemed to go on and on. Ken's heart raced and his mind filled with thoughts of what it would be like to be trapped in the rubble if this massive building collapsed. Finally, the shaking subsided.

He began to hear doors open and shut, so he got dressed and went downstairs. The lobby was full of other guests and some even meandered out on the lawn, but no one seemed to be panicked. After a tense 45 minutes, he finally went back upstairs to try to sleep. He learned the next day that the quake registered 4.6.

In one of the smaller towns near a cliff overlooking a spectacular valley, Ken found a whole group of plastic shanties. Little naked brown children, soaking wet from a bath, clamored all over the cross. A family of seven invited him to come inside their dwelling and Ken ducked under the plastic covering and sat with them.

One of the girls with a beautiful and bright countenance began to weep. She explained to Ken that they were Christians and had been praying for help to come. They were discouraged because they had heard some help had reached the next town, but then the aid had run out and there was nothing left to bring to their town.

Days had passed. Then she said she saw Ken approaching with the cross and she felt like it was a sign that God had truly not forgotten them. Ken prayed with this sweet family and gave them bags of milk, rice, and beans. He then sat under their flimsy covering and encouraged them for a long while.

There was story after story like this from his time in El Salvador. But soon his week was up and he headed to the airport to board his plane for home. He would be leaving this "land of the swinging hammocks" as the locals call it, but these precious people would all have to stay and work through this tragedy in their lives.

He couldn't help but feel relieved though, to be leaving all the rumbling under his feet that had accompanied him the last seven days. He was standing by the glass window, hoping to watch them load his luggage, especially to make sure the cross got into the aircraft. He remembered uttering thanksgiving to God in prayer for His faithful protection. Not ten seconds later, a big quake struck. Pandemonium broke out! People began screaming and scrambling for some kind of cover.

The lady next to Ken dropped to her knees and began screaming and praying in Spanish. Most of the people in the terminal were panicked. People were praying and calling upon the name of the Lord at full volume. Unlike most tremors that had come and gone rather quickly, this one seemed to intensify and go on and on.

Many people charged the only exit they could see—the jet way. At first the gate attendant tried to resist them, but the more the building shook and the tremor lingered, she finally let everyone that wanted go into the jet way. Plaster fell from the walls, ceiling tiles tumbled down, and dust filled the air as people continued yelling and praying.

Finally, after about 40 seconds, the ground and building quit shaking. People around Ken were confused and panicked, but Ken said unlike the nighttime quake, he had perfect peace. It was like he watched the whole thing through a camera view finder. He knew this was because of all the prayers back home.

For the next 15 or 20 minutes, tension hung in the air as everyone waited to see if the boarding of the airplane would proceed. They didn't know whether or not the whole airport would be closed. Fireman in all their gear walked about checking for damage and they finally indicated that everything was okay.

When the time came to board the aircraft, people couldn't care less about seating row instructions and just moved or pushed their way into the jet way. The gate attendant was fine with that too, quickly taking boarding passes and letting people go by. It was apparent the air crew were just as eager to leave.

Ken was also glad to be out from under the concrete buildings and was relieved to feel the airplane take off and leave this shaking ground. The last quake he was in at the airport had registered 6 on the Richter scale.

When Ken returned, he shared the stories of the people he had met and talked to during his week in El Salvador. They had many, many Christians praying for them as they slowly put their lives back together.

~11~
European Road Trip

The year was 2001. We are always fine-tuning our travel and searching for the best and least expensive way to get around. I booked our upcoming trip through a company online that offered airfare and car rental for a specific price. It seemed a good deal. We would make a huge circle around Europe, basing in Germany and visiting five countries. Ken would again carry the life-size wooden cross in the main city centers.

I'm sure with GPS now, this kind of travel is much easier, but we found it to be a huge headache. And with train passes and the ease of European public transport, we have since decided *never again!* There were advantages, like traveling on our own timetable and being able to have more luggage (like our ski-bag with the cross), but we found public transport to be much easier.

This trip had come together pretty well, but as we prepared to leave for our two months in Germany we were very short of funds. The plane ticket and car rental was purchased, but we left with very little cash. We didn't feel it was wise to lose what we had already paid, so we got on the plane trusting God to provide our needs while we were in Germany.

We started our trip with friends who live in a small village called Eckelsheim. Ken worked with Jean-Pierre when he lived in Germany in the early eighties. We always try to visit them when in Germany.

Usually while we are in Eckelsheim, Ken is asked to preach at a unique church in nearby Wollstein. Most of the churches in Germany are state churches and not very relevant to today. So we were glad to be connected with this small evangelical church. Before we left, Ken was asked to speak to their "teenies." He did so and we also spent time with the youth leader and prayed for her over some areas.

When we got back to our friends' house around eight o'clock, there was a knock on the door. It was the youth leader we had just left. She handed our friend an envelope for us and then slipped back out the door. We looked in it and it was $1,000! We had received small offerings from the churches Ken had preached in at times, but this was the first (and only) time our support ever came through a German donor.

As we tried to go to sleep that night, jetlag was still keeping us up at night and sleepy during the day. I couldn't go to sleep and after Ken had slept for about an hour, he was also wide awake. We talked for a while, read to each other out loud, and even got up and ate a snack we had in our room. I remember we were so tired we laughed and giggled at nothing. Ken began to read to me again and I finally got sleepy around 3:30 am. He later told me he also went back to sleep about that time.

Nürnberg

We set out in our small rental car, with the cross pieces between us sticking up from the back. Our first stop on our around Europe tour was in Nürnberg, Germany. I felt more bold this year about going out with Ken and had decided to talk to people with my small amount of German and hopefully encounter people who spoke English. Before leaving, I had found this scripture and felt it was instruction for me: "Whatever a person is like, I try to find common ground with him so that he will let me tell him about Christ and let Christ save him" 1 Corinthians 9:22b (LB).

As we drove into the city of Nürnberg, I had the map and a hotel book, searching for one nearest the FGZ. We saw one I had found in the book, but spotted it just as Ken went by it. Ken pulled into a parking place, and since we were not sure if we could park there, I ran back to the hotel and got us a room. The hotel had a parking garage, so I then ran back to where Ken was waiting and we pulled into the garage.

Even in our small economy car, we had trouble maneuvering into these small, compact garages. Sometimes it seemed as if we would surely scrape the sides of the walls. We are used to *everything is bigger in Texas*, but we found that *everything is smaller in Europe*. We even had one garage that was made with a lift-system. We drove our car onto the metal framework and then pushed a button and it rotated down below ground level. Another car could be pulled in that would literally be on top of ours. It reminded me of a huge vending machine!

When we got to our room on the fifth floor, we looked out and we could see the old city wall built between the 12th and 16th centuries. Four of the original five kilometers of the wall still stand. Inside one of the gates was the center of the city and the FGZ, where we would go the next day with the cross.

The next morning, we put the cross together for the beginning walk on this trip. We are always a little nervous the first time and as the three pieces of wood became a cross, we stood and *in Jesus' name* began walking toward the gate. Once inside the wall, we headed for one of the market squares.

At the center of one of the main squares was a statute called *Ehekarussell* or Marriage Carousel. It depicted couples in different life situations, but was completely weird and even somewhat lewd. So for that reason we referred to it as the debauchery statue. The artist obviously had a strange idea of marriage!

We were able to share with several people, including many teens. People who were drawn to look at the statue soon became small crowds that Ken was able to speak to about the saving grace of Jesus. He talked to one older gentleman for several minutes and felt he received the message of the cross.

We parked the cross here for some time and talked to people. They were, as Jesus called them, *sheep without a shepherd.* As we looked into their eyes, all we could see was emptiness. This compelled us to reach out to the people here in this infamous former Nazi city.

If you see old newsreels of Hitler standing before his massive army as they march by, it was likely filmed here in Nürnberg. Hitler staged his huge Nazi rallies here and exalted over all this power from a stage set up to look out over his troops. Once this regime had fallen, the trials for these sadistic war criminal leaders were also held in this city, simply called the Nürnberg Trials. In an irony of history, the city that had made the laws stripping the Jews of their citizenship, then later hosted the trials for the judgment of the remaining Nazi party leaders.

As we left this area, another older man stands out in my mind. He stopped and began asking Ken what this was all about. As Ken started giving his testimony, he began to laugh very loud. He turned and went on down the street, still laughing exaggeratingly loud. Sometimes this pure mockery is startling, but doesn't affect us. I felt sorry for him and prayed for him as he went his way. He had turned down a chance to hear of a Savior who offered him eternal life.

Prague

We continued our journey by heading to our next country, the Czech Republic. As we drove along in our rental car in the old city of Prague, I was the navigator. Before we left home, I had printed out a map and knew just how to get to the room we had rented online. This was before GPS was in everyone's car or pocket, so we had to follow a map. But as soon as we crossed the bridge into the old part of Prague, we encountered trouble. The street that was supposed to lead us to our room was under construction. And as happens often in Europe, the street was completely closed to through traffic.

As we were carried a completely different way by the traffic flow, I desperately started looking for another street we could take. There are not many places in Europe to just pull over and check the map. Parking is always premium and usually not available. Unlike America, where there are plenty of places to pull over, like parking lots, to get your bearings or turn around, European streets are not user friendly for drivers. Tons of traffic and mostly one-way streets means if you miss a turn or cannot locate a street, the flow of traffic pushes you miles out of the way. It is a nightmare if you're not familiar with the city!

By the time I would locate a street with names like *Bartolomějská* or *Masarykovo nábř* and try to read it off to Ken, we would already be past it. We involuntarily visited much of the city that day as we backtracked time and again until we finally spotted what looked like a small parking lot. We pulled in to catch our breath and our bearings. As we looked at our map, we realized we were in walking distance of our hotel and the parking garage was just a few yards away. We parked the car, where we gladly left it for the duration of our trip.

As we walked with the cross into a park the next day, Ken headed for a group of young people lounging around on the beautiful lawn. Ken tried to communicate with them in English or German, but they kept insisting "only Czech." Ken kept pressing in with English (which I'm sure they understood), when an earnest young man named Thomas walked up and asked Ken if he was making fun of the cross.

Since this young man was intensely interested in spiritual things, Ken then centered on him for over an hour.

Thomas had accepted an Eastern religion and claimed he had his turnaround to religion a year before. But he claimed this had all happened while he was high on LSD. Ken presented him with the truth of the gospel.

Thomas did not turn his life over to God that day, but I prayed much for him, depending upon the convicting power of the Holy Spirit. I felt encouragement in my heart that he at last had heard (and listened) to the truth. And I knew that truth could stand against the counterfeits.

We walked on from the park to the Old Town Square. It was huge and we always feel a little awed as we walk onto these city centers where people gather to eat, shop, or just hang out. There are all kinds of things going on to draw one's attention, including people singing or playing instruments for money. It usually doesn't take long for Ken to engage in conversation with people, so we walked around, talking and witnessing to different ones.

There were so many tourists and visitors that at one point I had to pick up the back of the cross and carry it to get safely through the crowds. We also saw lots of policemen. A friend of mine had given me some *sage* advice for dealing with any policemen we happen to encounter while walking the cross. She said, *Just walk fast!* So we took Sandy's advice at that moment and just kept walking – fast.

We had a couple of well-dressed kids come up to us with their Dixie cups held out begging for money. We ignored the cups and talked to them. We saw them off and on the rest of the day and had a fun time with them.

As we stood at one point, waiting to see who we would talk to next, a British lady came up to us and asked, *What time is your next show?* We weren't quick enough on our feet to say, *Oh, in about 5 minutes!*

In preparation for this trip, we had made tracts and books to give to people. Our friend, Jean-Pierre had helped in the translation of our book on the cross to German. We were handing out a few of these when we were stopped. We didn't have time to "walk fast" and were busted! It was the Czech police. We didn't know what we had done wrong, but expected to at least be thrown off the square. We didn't speak any Czech, but thankfully the policeman spoke a little German and we were able to communicate with him.

He thought we were selling the books we were passing out. We assured him we were not! He stood there holding one of our books for a moment and then said, "But this is not official." As we stood waiting for whatever decision he was going to make, he looked at Ken, smiled, and said, "Can I keep this?" We gladly told him yes, with a prayer that it would be life-changing for him. At that point, all was okay. In fact, he seemed pleased to have our Jesus book!

It is hard to convey all the conversations we have, but one was particularly interesting. We were on a street corner, and were stopped by a couple of young men. One was Czech and the other was from Slovenia, who was especially interested. As we talked to him, we realized we had no language in common with him. He spoke neither English nor German. Ken would speak English to the Czech man and he would translate what was said to the Slovenian. At times they would speak to each other, trying to get the full meaning of what Ken was saying. This three-way conversation went on for about 30 minutes.

Toward the end of our stay in Prague, we decided to eat at a small outdoor café, just at the foot of the Charles Bridge. It was a memorable place and we enjoyed the ambiance. But it also took on a totally different atmosphere when over the speakers we heard the 1969 hit by Kenny Rogers, *Ruby, Don't Take Your Love to Town*. We could hardly eat out dinner for laughing. It was so funny to hear this bit of corny Americana coming to us in the Czech language.

As the lights started coming on in this great city, we walked back across the Charles Bridge to our room. Many vendors and attractions were set up on the famous bridge. We stopped at one of these where a man was "playing" music by tapping glasses filled with different degrees of water. The bridge itself was a museum with 30 different statues built into the bridge. The one that sticks in my memory is of First Century Christians imprisoned in a cave with bars across the front. They are in different positions of prayer, but with agony on their faces, as if they are about to be martyred for their faith.

The drive out of Prague was even worse than the drive in. We could not get out! When we would finally locate a street on the map, it would be one-way, going the wrong way. So we again saw much more of Prague that morning then we intended. After a very frustrating hour we finally found our road and headed north to Germany and the former East German city of Dresden. We were soon to find out our driving troubles were not over for the day, but just beginning.

Dresden

As we got closer to Dresden, I pulled out my array of maps that I had printed from the Internet before leaving home. We try to always stay in a group of hotels called *Ibis* when traveling in Europe. They are reasonable and we always know what they will generally look like. From our hotel book, we saw that there were three Ibis buildings in a row, each 11 or 12 stories high. How hard could they be to find, right? As soon as we entered Dresden we spotted them, sticking up like signposts in this part of the city.

As before in Prague, we started running into one-way streets and even part of the blocked-off FGZ as we tried to get near the structures, which we could easily see. And one street on the map was simply not there anymore. We circled around and around the hotel, but could not find a way to the parking. We called the hotel lobby twice and they tried to lead us in, but the directions seemed overwhelming. I'm sure our minds were on full overload by this time and it was hard to even comprehend what the hotel clerks were saying.

Once again after an hour long "unwanted" city tour, we finally found the entrance to the parking lot only to find it was full. We knew from experience to just turn the car off, and wait for someone to exit to take their place. After about ten minutes, a car came out and we were allowed in to find the one empty parking place. Exhausted and overwhelmed, we finally got to our room.

The three tall buildings were built in 1969, and from the outside looked like some kind of former East Germany housing blocks. I could never find any verification on this, but if they had been built for this purpose, they were now modern, stylish hotels. It had only been 12 years since German reunification and we were beginning to see signs of modernization. The communist powers-that-be that had controlled this city for more than forty years had been content to leave the city for the most part like it was after the war—broken down and weary-looking. We were to see signs of this for ourselves later on.

On our quest for hotels, we always tried to get as close to our target, the FGZ, as possible. When we walked out the front door of our Ibis hotel, we were on the FGZ. So for all the trouble getting here, it was perfect for our outreach to this city. After we ate dinner, Ken went for a walk up the FGZ to pray and get focused after our hectic day of travel.

After a good rest, we were ready to go the next morning. After our breakfast, I ventured out on my own to get us water for the day and to buy postage stamps. For some reason, it was too daunting for me. The Germans have a reputation for being all-business, even to the point of rudeness, and I didn't think I could face an impatient German civil-servant. Ken even agreed with me when I got back that he should probably help me with this.

This attitude has changed since I have been going to Germany. They are more customer-friendly and will speak English to tourists. This is probably because of all the changes that have come to Germany over the last several years. For one thing, they are not inundated with young

American soldiers who, for many, did not leave a good impression on the people.

As the generations get further removed from the war years, their opinion of Americans has also improved. Before we were married, Ken had lived in Germany in 1982. He grew a beard and tried to fit in to looking and sounding like a German so he could blend in more naturally. Now that is less important because it is *cool* for Germans to talk to Americans, and especially for the young people to try out their English.

This was particularly true for the former East Germany. They seemed more appreciative of their new lifestyle and more willing to please the tourists and visitors to their land. They were also out from behind the dark wall of communism and were able to travel and meet people from other countries. They were much friendlier than their counterparts in the West.

As we walked onto the FGZ with the cross, we decided to try harder to break through the natural reserve of people meeting a stranger. We wanted to disarm people, so walked along enthusiastically waving and smiling at everyone we met. Our new motto we began here was "Be winsome to win some." And it really seemed to work. The happiness we had seemed to spread to those around us. There are always some who mock, but most were joyful with us and appreciated what we were doing.

Young teenagers seemed particularly drawn to Ken and the cross. They would walk up to him in groups and stand there while he explained what he was doing and why. These were kids who had been small children when their country changed so dramatically. We knew we were a part of all the new experiences they were being flooded with and wanted the gospel to stand out in their minds. We were always able to put literature in their hands as they left us to catch their bus or move along.

But we also had a few chances to minister to some of the older people. One such man told Ken he was an atheist and believed that Jesus was only a legend. Ken explained to him all the historical manuscripts (including many, many secular historians and even Roman government officials) that have been discovered about Jesus. He was visibly taken aback and had no answer to this. Ken was able to put a book in his hand that we hoped would further show him that Jesus was anything but a legend.

We were a little hindered in this great city because of a celebration that was to take place the following day. They were having a huge ceremony at the Cathedral of the Holy Trinity Church, celebrating 250 years of Catholicism in Dresden. It seemed people thought we were part of this ceremony and made some keep their distance.

The great cathedral was in the middle of a huge square just next to the Elbe River. We took the cross up a small incline to a park overlooking the square and the river. Just below us was the Augustus Bridge crossing the beautiful river. As we sat there eating our bratwurst lunch, Ken began talking to an older man. It was one of those conversations that has stuck with me all these years and touched my heart very deeply.

In February of 1945, Dresden was heavily bombed for two straight days. The bombs and resulting firestorm destroyed much of the city center and killed around 25,000 people. The man who sat before us telling his story was a young boy on one of those horrific nights and was actually in the square we were looking down on with his grandmother. The church was hit and the roof taken off. He and his grandmother ran across the square and tried to get across the bridge to flee the fires all around them.

As the two started across the bridge, he looked down at one point and saw the phosphorous from the bombs lighting up the water and realized there were massive holes in the bridge. If he hadn't looked down, his next step would have been into the Elbe River. They turned around and made it back to the square where they were able to get to safety. It was a somber moment as we sat there in the bright sunshine eating our picnic, overlooking the very bridge and square he was talking about, and remembering what had happened to this man so many years ago.

He told us that all the rebuilding that was going on had only been in the last 10 years – since the fall of communism. The communists promised to rebuild but never did. All they built were (what he called) ugly apartment buildings. The Dresden he had known before the war had been called the *Florence on the Elbe* and had once been very beautiful with its old styles and buildings.

We had seen some of this initiative ourselves. As we walked through the old city center, we actually still saw crumbled walls of old buildings waiting to be refurbished. Many new shops and restaurants were being added, trying to restore some of the beautiful ambiance of former times.

As we walked back through this great city, we also came across the rebuilding of the grand Lutheran church, the *Dresdner Frauenkirche*. It was built in the 18th Century as a Roman Catholic church called *Church of Our Lady*. It became Protestant during the Reformation and was destroyed in the bombing in 1945. It was under construction as we walked by it and has since been finished and was reopened in 2005.

We walked back toward our hotel around 6:00 pm that evening and took the cross apart and put it back in our car. We went back outside to join the people out on the FGZ and market squares who were grabbing quick bites to eat or just enjoying an evening stroll. As we sat down on a bench, eating our *Doner Kabobs* (Turkish sandwiches in Pita bread), two young men came and sat down and began to ask Ken about the cross.

We recognized them and remembered that they had laughed at us earlier, so were a little skeptical and not sure of their motive. But they listened as Ken gave them his testimony. We have found we can never discount the mockers. It is not always true, but sometimes those who protest the loudest are the ones being convicted and drawn the most by God's Spirit.

The next day, we started out on the FGZ and were in for a shock. There were no people and shops everywhere were closed. It was a German holiday, and like Sundays, the whole city comes to a halt. It was eerily quiet and we realized there would not be any crowds of people out and about. There are so many more German holidays than in the United States, and we encountered this several more times on our trip. We were thankful for the rest at times, but hindered with our outreach.

We were headed for Berlin the next day. As we packed our car and made ready to leave, we prayed together and asked God to lead us this day. We didn't want any more of the stressful confusion that had plagued us on our arrivals in Prague and Dresden. We made the two hour trip fine and headed for our villa!

Berlin

As soon as we arrived back in Germany from the Czech Republic, we had begun making calls to hotels in Berlin to find a room. Ken was scheduled to preach in a church there the following Sunday. We were a little worried that all the Ibis hotels seemed to be full. So we ventured out to others that we knew of. Then we started calling all the hotels listed in the phone book. Not only did they say they had no rooms, they kept telling us there were **no** rooms in all of Berlin available!

We found this a little hard to believe. Berlin was a big city. How could it be completely full! Finally someone informed us of the problem. There was a soccer championship happening that weekend which was equivalent to our Super Bowl. The Chancellor of Germany, Gerhard Schröder, would even be in attendance, giving out the trophy at the end.

In our quest, we had come across a single room available. We knew this would probably just be a small, twin-size bed, but we were desperate and called back to see if we could have that room. They then told us they had had a cancellation and now had a double room available!

We found the address that was given us and pulled up before a beautiful estate with what was at one time an Italian villa with a beautiful lawn in a residential area. This was so different from our Ibis hotel rooms that were always nice and clean, but usually very small and modern.

When we walked into our room, my mouth literally fell open. It was all done in Victorian style, with pinks and whites. There was a huge window covering one whole wall overlooking one of the water gardens. The room had a classic high ceiling and even a chandelier. It looked like a magazine picture!

The next day, we took the train into downtown Berlin with gospel tracts. We knew there would be crowds of people for the soccer match, which made it hard to maneuver even walking, much less if we had the cross. But we had no idea when we started just what this would look like. We were overwhelmed with literal hordes of people!

There were groups of mostly young men dressed either in blue or red, the team colors from the two sides playing for the championship. Many had wigs on with the same color. On one end of the city, there was a red parade, with people getting ready for the big game.

Ken wanted to take me to the main part of Berlin, to show me some of the places he had visited before. The train we were on was very crowded, but as we pulled into the underground Berlin Zoo station for our stop, hundreds of people dressed in blue were crowded on the narrow platform to board our train. It was time to head for the stadium and thousands of people all over the city were straining to literally cram onto the trains.

I had never been in this kind of crowds before and it was very unnerving. As we pushed our way out of the train, it was immediately packed before the whistle blew and the train took off down the track. I didn't see how people could even move in the cars that went by. I was so glad we were off the train, but we still had to thread our way through the crowd still waiting and up the stairs to daylight.

As we walked around the areas Ken had wanted to show me, including Ku'Dam Platz (marketsquare), there were still huge crowds everywhere. This had obviously been the meeting place for the blue team. There was trash and beer bottles everywhere and it reeked of urine. All this totally changed the look of this famous square that is so often depicted on post cards of Berlin.

The Ku'Dam Platz surrounds the *Kaiser-Wilhelm-Gedächtniskirche* (Kiser Wilhelm Memorial Church). Its spire had been damaged during the bombing in 1943 and left unrepaired as a memorial. We quickly toured the square then decided to go on to *Potsdamer Platz* (Potsdam Square), which we hoped would be quieter.

I had visited Berlin in 1990 and 91 but had not been back since the rebuilding had taken place in the former East Berlin. The spot we were standing had been *no man's land* just twelve years before. It was the infamous area between the wall the communists had erected in East Berlin and the walls and barbed wire fences built right on the West Berlin border.

Since there had been no buildings in this area, a new, modern city square was built out of the ignoble place it had been. It was surreal to see the huge sky-scrapers and contemporary buildings in the middle of this old city.

We made our way back to our room that night, flipped on our TV, and watched some of the game being played in another part this great city. We saw the huge crowds in the stadium and understood why we had been told there were no rooms left in Berlin!

As Ken preached the following day in our friend's church, we were greatly ministered to by the worship. It was so good to be among other Christians and refill our empty spiritual tanks. I felt so refreshed. When we are on the road like this for weeks at a time, it is so good to be with God's people to get recharged and ready to go back out.

Stralsund

We drove from Berlin to the very tip of northeast Germany, the town of Stralsund and the nearby island of Rügen. We based out of Stralsund and drove onto the island the next morning and headed to the city of Bergen. As soon as we walked onto a small square with the cross, we were surrounded by seven 12-year olds. We talked and shared with them for about an hour. As before, we realized these former East Germany kids had just been born in 1989 and had no idea what the wall was all about that had separated their parents from the rest of the world.

We did get one glimpse of how cut off this part of the world had been when Ken opened his Bible to read something to them. They all gathered up close and stared at the pages with awe and told us they had never seen inside a Bible before. One of them said his grandmother had one but we could tell it was a mysterious and probably still secret world for them. I'm sure anyone who had a Bible during the communist days had had to hide it. It was probably not easy for these older people to change those habits and openly read their Bibles.

After we had talked to them for a while, they started drifting off, saying they had to catch their bus home. It was getting late, but one boy remained. He told Ken, "I have time." I will never forget the face of that young boy as Ken continued to explain the gospel to him and talk about Jesus. He was soaking it in like a dry sponge. He was trying to figure everything out and at one point asked Ken how he could put his faith in Jesus. What a privilege to explain a wonderful Savior to this hungry young person.

We drove back to our hotel in Stralsund, which was right on one of the main squares. After a quick dinner at McDonald's, we walked to an area by our parking lot where kids were skateboarding. Ken was able to preach to about 20 of them and give them books on the cross. They were very quiet and attentive and said they would read the books.

The next day, we went downstairs to check out of our hotel. When we looked out on the square, it was covered with different vendors, from meat and vegetable stands to rows of beautiful cut flowers and bouquets. It was market day.

We had a moment of panic, because the market was being held on the very parking lot we had parked our rental car. We didn't see it at first for all the vendor wagons, but found it just where we had parked. In fact, Ken had moved it to the second row to be closer to the hotel the night before. We saw a sign that said any cars that were parked beyond the second row on market day would be towed! We praised God all day for leading Ken to move the car, even when he had no idea God was leading him.

Rostock

We drove to our next city on our circular tour, which was Rostock. We found our Ibis hotel quickly and were checked in and ready to go at noon. We had met such friendly people in Stralsund that we were a little stunned at the reception in this town. It was different than Stralsund in that it seemed more metropolitan, not as laid-back as the harbor town where we'd just been. They had obviously just renovated the whole city center, which was very beautiful with colorful facades all around. But it had the complete air of worldliness.

Even when the adults are stand-offish, Ken can usually engage young people. We came to a small park with groups of teenagers sitting around. Ken tried to talk to several of these groups, but no one was interested. He talked to a few people and put books in their hands, but for the most part, Rostock seemed the epitome of Matthew 10:14, "If any household or town refuses to welcome you or listen to your message, shake its dust from your feet as you leave" (NLT). We left this city grieved in our hearts that for the most part, no one seemed interested in listening to our message.

Amsterdam

We circled the northern tip of Germany, stopping in different cities like Wismar and Bremen (doing little ministry because of yet more unknown German holidays) on our way to our third country, the Netherlands. We drove to Amsterdam and checked into an Ibis by the airport. We could take the free shuttle to the airport, then ride the train to the city center.

Once in the city, Ken put the cross together and then we walked onto the great *Dam Square*, just a few minutes' walk from the main train station. We were standing on the very square that Napoleon and his troops rode onto in 1808 as they took over the city.

Ken climbed the steps around the National Monument Statue (built in 1956 to commemorate those killed in World War II) and began interacting with the dozens of young people congregated there. That's the beauty of carrying a life-sized cross; people are always curious and he soon had a group surrounding him.

As we walked around this great city, it was clear they were

very intent on going their own way and not following God. They had legalized marijuana and prostitution and drew in people from all over the world who wanted to follow after evil. As Ken walked with the cross, one older man who was obviously filled with demons came up to us seething and shouting obscenities against God. I have never seen such hate and rage against God. It was quite a lesson in progressive thinking and showed us the cesspool life becomes when all restraints are thrown away.

We walked around this great city with its canals dissecting the city like streets. We even took a boat ride around the canals and saw the house where Anne Frank spent her two years locked away in hiding and then was eventually taken away and murdered. Such dark history in this now modern city.

Brussels

We turned our sights toward our fourth country, Belgium. We had met a young couple in Azle, Texas at a Promise Keeper's Breakfast. They had invited us to stay at their house in Namur and we looked forward to being with them again.

Namur is a beautiful city just outside of Brussels, with the rivers Sambre and Meuse converging there. A castle overlooked the confluence of these two rivers.

They had a lovely home that seemed huge after our small accommodations in Europe. They had built it themselves and we saw a southwest flair with their spacious rooms and tile floors. But as we shared and grew close to this couple, we realized they were already in the process of leaving all this behind. They desperately wanted to move to America, because of all the suffocating liberalism descending on their country that was taking away their religious freedoms. It seems so easy to take for granted the freedoms we have. It is also scary to realize how quickly they can be snatched away from us.

(They finally made it to America years later by a tedious, circular route. Because of bureaucracy I can't even begin to understand, they first had to move to Canada, then after a few years were permitted to settle in America. The last we heard, they were working with a ministry here in Texas.)

Their pastor came by to meet us, since Ken would be preaching at their church the next day in Brussels. He was a jolly man and very friendly. This was so different from the reactions we receive in other parts of Europe from older people who went through the war. He was so thankful for America and the part they had played. He said they would all be speaking German or Russian, if not for America! He knew that America was not interested in taking over countries, but rather helping to liberate them.

Before we left, we were invited to his farm for lunch one day. He was very proud of his small acreage of farmland and said it was a blessing from God. We sat down to our usual two hour meal as he fed us chicken from his own brood. The meals always included dessert at the end and were not finished until the coffee was served. Even if the meals were simple, they never seemed in a hurry and followed this same pattern.

We rode through our fifth country, the small country of Luxembourg which is only about 1,000 square miles total. We drove from Namur to Koblenz in Germany in about four hours and were in three different countries!

Koblenz

We found our next Ibis hotel easily and were glad to discover the FGZ close by and also a laundry right across the street. The city of Koblenz is also a confluence of two rivers, the Rhine and Mosel. Overlooking where these two rivers converge is the *Deutsches Eck* (German Corner) with an enormous statue of the Emperor William the Great on horseback. This is a huge tourist attraction, so we headed there with the cross.

Ken had many good conversations with people and at one point hoisted the cross up the steps of the statue to talk to a group of students who were shouting and mocking him. He went into the fray and talked to them for a long time. There were no outward signs that day of acceptance of his words, but we believe God's word and His Holy Spirit works in hearts once they are away from their peers.

I also had one of what I have begun calling my *bench ministry* days. After walking with Ken a while I usually drift over to a bench and sit to take pictures, pray, and rest. Invariably, I find someone to talk to. This day was no different and an older woman asked me the time of day. With the ice broken, I began to communicate with her in my limited German. When Ken came along from the statue steps, I motioned for him to come and talk to her. We talked for some time and Ken was able to put a book in her hands.

When we awoke the next morning, I noticed how quiet the city streets were. Sure enough, it was another holiday— one of many for our time in Germany. The streets are eerily deserted, which means no people to talk to! This was our last day for ministry with the cross, so was frustrating. We decided to take a tourist day, and went for a short boat ride up the Mosel. It is very beautiful in this area, whether on the Rhine or Mosel. There are castles on most of the mountain tops and it was a very peaceful ride.

Andernach

Our next outreach was the beginning of a relationship with a group of precious young people that is still going on today. We were on our way to Andernach, just up from Koblenz on the Rhine River. We were meeting a group of almost 50 Americans to do a youth camp and then a basketball camp. We didn't have a clue what this would look like and didn't realize we were getting ready to witness some of the greatest miracles of the whole trip.

The youth camp was not like anything we have here in the states. There were a few Christians from the church, but most of the attendees were un-churched young people. The camp was set up with a big central tent for the meetings and meals with smaller tents all around for sleeping. There was a soccer field nearby for the sports camp part of the camp and other smaller tents for breakout sessions.

One of my jobs during the camp was, of all things, washing dishes. The Germans use very few paper products, so we had a commercial type dishwasher brought in and stacked and washed hundreds of dishes after each meal. I was astounded after the first breakfast at all the dishes. I should have realized our proper Germans would all use a plate, cup **and** saucer, fork, knife, and spoon even if they were at camp!

We were all-hands-on-deck for the whole weekend, serving refreshments, holding breakout sessions, or just hanging out with the kids on the soccer field. Ken was able to preach in a couple of the main sessions and was honored to be able to give the main evangelistic appeal on the last night.

As I think about the results of this first youth camp with City Church of Andernach, I can't help but think about one young man who was greatly influenced and his life totally changed. His name was Kenneth and I'll let him tell you in his own words what happened during Jesus Camp.

Kenneth: I was born in Moldova, one of the former Soviet Republics just above the Black Sea. My parents split up when I was five. My dad went back to Africa and my mom and I moved to Germany.

Later when I became a teenager I got into drugs. At the beginning, I only played with drugs. At first it was a lot of fun and my friends and I laughed a lot. When we took these drugs, it was to party. Then came the point when the friendship was no longer in the middle—the drugs were. What really became important were the drugs.

At that point I had dropped out of school. I had no apartment, no job—I had nothing except these drugs. And I was really, really down and broke. I was looking for a way out but I couldn't find any. I wanted to leave my friends, but really there was nowhere to go. I thought, *Where can I go?*

Then one day I was in the city and I was smoking and stoned. I was on the way back to my house when I met Mike and Damir (some of City Church's leaders). They spoke with me about a youth camp with people from America and invited me to come. When I heard there would be Americans there that was the only thing I was interested in—not Mike, not Damir, not youth camp. I was interested in America—the things you see on TV like beautiful cars and beautiful girls. That's the only reason I went.

I said yes and I used the last money I had. It was about 80 Deutsch Marks ($40), and I went to the camp. In all the pockets of my pants, I had enough weed to smoke at the camp every day.

There were a lot of little tents to sleep in and there was a big tent where we would have the services. And then I noticed there were rules for the camp. No alcohol and no drugs.

On the first evening, I went into the big tent. First there were these rules and now they started to "worship." The people stood up and began to sing and raise their hands. Then a girl beside me started to cry. It was everything new for me. And I thought *These people are crazy!* After I got outside the tent I thought, *Ok, I'm going to check out these American girls now.* I went up to some of the girls and said, *Hello, how are you doing?* I wanted to pick them up, but it didn't work.

Then someone talked about the Bible and that this was a Christian camp. At that point I realized for the first time this *is* a Christian camp. I think the guys had told me that, but I didn't really get it. I didn't pay attention. All I heard was "America." So I was really, really mad. I gave my last money to a Christian camp! I would have gladly given it for drugs, for parties, for such dumb things like that. But not for a Christian camp!

I was upset with Damir and Mike. But I stayed at the camp. Even though I was mad about the money and I was mad at Damir and Mike, I wanted to show them that I was strong and I was really a man. But I also want to make the point that the camp was fun too. I was having a really good time, so not everything was bad.

Then we came into the big tent again and there was a preacher. He spoke exactly about my life—like he was talking to me. And I thought, *Has he been watching me?* And I couldn't believe this. How can this one man who doesn't know me speak about me and my life? I thought maybe they had cameras or something. But he knew things he wouldn't be able to know.

We came to the last day of the camp—the last service in the big tent. As I came into the tent that night, I just wanted to hide. I didn't want anyone to see me stand up and worship and do all that holy stuff. Even though I wanted to hide, as soon as I walked in the tent, this girl said, *Hey Kenneth, come sit here!*

That night it was all the same kind of stuff—worshipping, praising the Lord. And then came the point at the end of the preaching when the leader said, *Jesus is standing before your heart. Jesus stands before your heart and knocks. Jesus knocks on your door. Do you hear that?* And I didn't get it. I looked around and I didn't see Jesus. I could not realize how Jesus could knock on my door. Then I thought, *Where is Jesus? These people have to be crazy!*

Then came the sentence, *Jesus is standing in front of you and He wants to come into your heart—into your life. He wants to change you.*

I said, *OK, all right then.* And then the music started and they said, *For two or three minutes we want you just to think about this. Then you can make this decision to stand up if you want to give your life to Christ.* I thought, *This is crazy. I will stay sitting. I won't do this!* And even inside I was laughing at all this. And then people around me started to stand up.

At this point I said I'm just going to sit back and relax. Then my heart started beating real hard. I took a breath and I thought, *What is wrong?* And I looked left and right to see if anybody could see what was happening to me.

It was like I was in a cinema. And I saw my entire life. It was like watching a movie—my drugs—my unemployment—everything. It was like watching everything bad that had happened. All the frustration. And I knew at this moment if I don't give my life to Jesus and keep persisting in this life, I'm going the wrong way. But if I give it to this Jesus, He will really take it. And then it was like I woke up. *OK, I can try it,* and I stood up.

At that moment I heard someone say, *Hey, look at Kenneth.* And I looked and it was an old friend of mine. I don't know how he got in the tent. It was a guy I knew who stole a lot of money from people in

Andernach. He was into drugs and everything; a really bad guy. He walked up to me and said, *What are you thinking? Are you crazy? Do you know what the Christians' rules are? No sex, no drugs, no alcohol, no partying.*

I was shocked. I wanted to sit back down. But at that moment the music stopped playing, and they said, *Those of you who are standing, come to the front. We want to pray with you.* Then I thought, *The best thing is to get out of here, run to my tent, grab my bag, and run away.*

But right at that moment people surrounded me and we all went forward to the platform. They actually hugged me up to the stage! Even though I wanted to be out of the tent, I found myself standing on the stage. And then everyone started to pray for me.

Then Mike came up and said, *Come on, I want to talk to you.* So we sat down and then Mike said, *I want to pray with you.* Then I said to Mike, *Don't pray with me. I heard the rules. No sex, no drugs, no parties. This is my life. I can't do that.* And Mike said, *When Jesus comes into your life, all that changes,* and he explained to me about old things passing away and all things becoming new. So I confessed to Mike everything that was bad in my life—everything that was holding me. He hugged me and prayed for me. And then he went away. And I thought, *That's it?*

Then came the moment that totally changed my life. I stood up and I felt funny like I could fly. And I thought, *What's the matter? I feel so funny. What is this? What is happening to me?* How can I describe this to you? Then I remembered what one of the preachers said: *Your old life is like an old heavy bag you used to carry. All your sins—all your bad life—all this stuff and Jesus is standing before your heart and He will take this bag away.*

Do you know this feeling? When you've carried something heavy for a long time? And then you laid it down? It's hard to describe what it was like. It was like my whole life had been in darkness and now a light came on. And I knew at that moment, Jesus is here! And I knew this is what I have searched for my whole life long. I found it in one man—Jesus Christ!

My life totally changed. I got rid of all my drugs. I went back to school. I had a new beginning.

Today...Kenneth is a leader in City Church and has a wife and sweet little girl. Every time I look at him, I know I am seeing the miracle of salvation. He is truly a new creation, the old is gone and the new has come (2 Corinthians 5:17)!

After the youth camp was finished on Monday morning, we all changed gears and went to the nearby city gym for the basketball camp. This would be a week of working with even more youth from the city. They came in droves to either participate in the basketball clinics or watch the games that were played.

While the basketball camp was going on, there was no official outreach but invitations were given out for a meeting at the church at the end of the week called *Crosspoint*. We'd had about a thousand kids at the basketball camp and exhibition, and more than 200 showed up for *Crosspoint*!

The church was decorated with army camouflage all over the walls and ceiling, with the stage arranged like an island. The theme of the meeting was *Survivor.* There were skits and a breakdance contest. It was almost 10:00 pm when Ken finally got the stage for the presentation of the gospel. By this time, the kids, who had no qualms about standing up and leaving an event, all started to do just that. Ken, in desperation to share the gospel with these young people we had been interacting with all week, fell on his knees and begged them to sit back down and listen.

And then an amazing thing happened. They all began to do as he asked. They sat and listened in hushed silence as Ken gave them the gospel, with the pastor of the church interpreting. It was an awesome night and one I'll never forget.

About 30 young people made first-time commitments to Christ during the two weeks we were in Andernach. To work hand in hand, side by side with so many others was a blessing beyond words.

We started our journey in Germany and made a huge circle through Germany and four other countries. We drove over 1500 miles and ministered in 18 cities in 58 days. We had ended it all by making friends with people that we still share ministry with to this day. What an incredible journey!

*"The man...looking at him with a smile that only
half concealed his contempt, inquired, "Now Mr.
Morrison do you really expect that you will make an
impression on the idolatry of the Chinese Empire?"
"No sir," said Morrison,
"but I expect that God will."*

~12~

Hearts for Germany!

*You mean we can go into the public schools and tell them about
Jesus?* The answer to this question was a resounding "Yes."
But we weren't here in good ole' America, but in the nation
of Germany. On one of our many trips to Germany, we were
invited to speak in several schools. The pastor who was
sponsoring us could not believe we couldn't do this in
America. But for us it was the chance of a lifetime.

One of these stops was to a school with one class of 14-
year olds and another with 15-year olds. Ken gave his
testimony and then talked to them about Jesus and what He
completed on the cross for them. He was able to speak about
40 minutes and then have them ask any questions they might
have. It was a wonderful time and Ken was able to connect
with them in an awesome way. As the bell rang for class to
end, they filed out but were still commenting on some of the
things that had been discussed and wanted to continue talking
to Ken.

Germany. Even though we go to many, many countries, this is the country that we feel the most called to go to. It is a beautiful land, with green, lush grass, hillsides full of vineyards and castles, and mighty rivers snaking through stunning scenery. It is also a very easy country to get around in. There is an excellent travel system that provides trains or busses almost anywhere we want to go.

It is also a land filled with history, from medieval castles to modern cities of war. Part of the cold war happened here, until the land was once again reunified in 1990. There is so much to see and do in this country.

But there is also something else in Germany. There are thousands and thousands of people who have never heard the gospel—once! They have heard about religion and know that some of their taxes go to the "church" whether they like it or not, but for the most part they have not been introduced to the real heart of the gospel—Jesus.

We here in America cannot conceive of it, but there are 250,000 cities and villages in Europe without a single evangelical church. There may be a church in a big city, but it is more museum and tourist attraction than church. People come to admire the glorious architecture of the building or attend an organ concert. But these multitudes visiting these churches virtually never hear the words of eternal life spoken by Jesus in the gospel or feel the least bit convicted of their sins. Often there are a few folding chairs off in one corner that the faithful still come to, but even that is for the older people and has very little life or vibrancy.

As we have travelled all over Germany time and again and spoken to thousands of people face to face and told them about the One who came to save their souls and to bring peace to this earth, they are usually stunned. They've never heard about Jesus and who He really is. We've had the priceless privilege of telling them of a Savior who has come to rescue them.

On one of our journeys in this land, we were walking the cross in some of the smaller villages around Andernach. Our driver, Robert, was a dear friend that we had known since first coming to this city to work in youth camps.

Robert took us to a village called Bad Neuenahr. It was February, a cloudy and windy day with misting rain. There were not very many people around, but we put the cross together and started up the street anyway. We talked to a few people, gave out some tracts, but for the most part it was a slow day.

We came upon a small bridge and stopped to look at the water below us. As we stood there gazing down, a TV crew came up behind us. As we turned around, we were face to face with a huge camera, and a reporter named Natasha who said she wanted to interview Ken.

They had taken us by surprise, so Ken had very little time to get his thoughts together. He also felt a little self-conscience about his German. He hoped he was getting his complex German grammar right and all his verbs in order. But it seemed to go well and he preached about Jesus in response to each question.

Steve, the cameraman then wanted to film Ken walking with the cross. They were gone a few minutes, so Robert was able to talk to Natasha. She said she had grown up Catholic and felt this would be a good story. Steve and Ken soon came back and they packed up and left us once again standing on the small bridge

We weren't sure if anything would come of it, but found out later the interview was broadcast on a regional newscast every half hour for two straight evenings. Many of the church people who saw it thought it was really great, so Natasha must have edited it well and allowed Ken to preach the gospel.

The pastor we were working with said it was nothing short of miraculous to have spoken about Jesus on the secular news and for the story to be cast in such a positive way.

So on a day that we thought was a "slow" day, God had arranged for Ken to speak into the lives of possibly hundreds of thousands of Germans!

There are many, many stories we could tell about our time in this nation. Sometimes we spend months there, going from city to city, preaching on the market squares. Other times, we've worked at youth camps, preached in churches, or hosted seminars. We've given out thousands of pieces of literature, tracts, and books. We've even had one of the books Ken has written about the cross translated into German. We've seen faces and countenances change as Ken has talked to them about the person of Jesus and explained the cross to them.

So our call to this land goes on and on. And I'm sure will continue through the years. It is in our hearts to shine the light of Jesus to these wonderful people.

*And people who do not know the Lord ask why in the world we
waste our lives as missionaries. They forget that they too are
expending their lives…and when the bubble has burst they will have
nothing of eternal significance to show for the years they have wasted.*
—Nate Saint

~13~
A Day Like No Other

Ken and I were sitting at the kitchen table, enjoying a leisurely breakfast with friends. We were in Memphis, Tennessee, on our way to North Carolina, stopping in different cities to do cross walks. We had no clue what a momentous and catastrophic day this would be by nightfall. It was 8:55 am and the date was September 11, 2001.

A dear friend I had roomed with in Texas had moved to Tennessee when she married. Her husband worked for FedEx. As we finished our breakfast, he was at the airport that morning waiting to catch a 9:00 flight to Los Angeles. He called a little before nine o'clock and said, "Something terrible has happened! Turn on the TV!"

We and her three small boys went into the den and did like most of America, flipped on the TV. We sat for hours, appalled, yet we couldn't take our eyes off what was happening right before us. We sat in shock as we watched a second plane fly into the World Trade Center. As the morning wore on, we were horrified to realize these were not empty planes with just terrorists on board, but planes full of ordinary people that had been hijacked in the air.

We didn't think it could get much worse and then we heard stories that people were jumping from the highest floors of the buildings to escape the fire raging behind them. We had no idea how many people were inside the buildings as we watched them crumble in on themselves into dust.

We wondered if this was going to start happening in every city across America as we heard of the Pentagon also being hit by a plane and the very mysterious occurrence of a plane flying over the Pennsylvania countryside out of its flight plan. The mystery was soon solved as we heard the tragic news of another plane crashing into a field. As the news kept unfolding, we learned of the stunning and heroic efforts of people on board that plane to crash it before it killed even more people.

As the day wore on, we learned that all the flights over America were cancelled and grounded. My friend's husband was thankfully was on his way home now instead of halfway across the nation. All international flights were diverted to Canada. The stock exchange closed and all government buildings were emptied and guarded. For those first moments, we were under siege and at war with an unknown enemy.

We had planned to go on to Nashville and stay with a friend who was in college there. Ken had planned a cross walk for the next day. For a while, we considered getting in our car and driving back to Texas. Everything seemed so uncertain. But as the hours went by and no further attack came, we decided to continue on with our trip.

It was strange traveling that day. I looked up at the sky and realized for the first time in *my* life, there were NO planes in the air. When we stopped to eat, the restaurant was subdued and quiet. It felt like we were in the middle of a huge funeral possession and no one wanted to talk above a whisper.

When we arrived in Nashville, our friend was not out of classes yet so we went to a nearby mall to pass the time. It was eerily quiet and we were some of the only customers. They finally announced over the loudspeaker that they were closing the mall and could everyone please exit. We had never seen anything like this, as the shops' security gates started closing all around us.

We finally connected with our friend and spent the evening trying to talk, but with one eye on the TV. It was still a waiting game to see if this was something bigger than what had already happened.

Ken continued with his cross walks as we made our way to North Carolina. He felt he needed to be out where the people were. Some people were glad to talk to him, others were withdrawn and quiet.

It was a strange week for our country. The nation seemed humbled and softened by what had happened. A small portion of our people had been attacked and we all took it as a personal thing, like it had happened to members of our family. People were caring for each other. Even the news media was different. They were being so careful in their reporting, sensitive and even crying at times.

I've never seen our nation so shut down, so preoccupied with the suffering going on in New York, Washington D.C., and Pennsylvania. There were no sports, no beauty pageants, no Emmy awards, and no regular TV programs at all from Tuesday to Sunday. It was like the whole nation took off work to attend a close family member's funeral.

Ken and a friend, Rex, left October 25, 2001 to fly to New York to carry the cross. I, like many in America, was not ready to get on an airplane yet. I knew this would not stop me from flying, but I had to let some of those images fade before I could fly again.

On their first day in New York, they took the subway down to lower Manhattan to check things out before taking the cross. They got off the subway about seven blocks from Ground Zero. They didn't know which way to go, but just began following the flow of people. Even at six blocks away it became apparent that they were headed in the right direction. The air was filled with particles of ash and they could already smell the acrid odor. Even after 45 days, the area was still smoldering.

As they came to within a couple of blocks, it became very confusing. They didn't know it at the time, but this was the very first day people were allowed to come that close to Ground Zero. The rules had not been established, and there were hundreds of people milling about with policemen and barricades on every corner. Not only were people from all over America there, but many New Yorkers, seeing the devastation for the first time. People were largely silent as they stared between buildings for glimpses of the scene.

They eventually wound up on a sidewalk near Trinity Church, less than a hundred yards from Ground Zero. A chain-link fence had become a makeshift memorial, with flowers and candles. By this time it was getting dark, and the glaring lights at the site made everything seem even more surreal.

Before leaving, they determined that they would be able to get the cross to this area, if the police did not intervene. They made their way back to the subway and to their hotel near Times Square.

They started out the next day with the cross in three pieces, strapped together and a backpack full of literature. Ken put it together once they were off the subway near Ground Zero. With a declaration of, *In Jesus' Name*, they walked into the fray of mankind in this tragic place. They passed several police checkpoints but no one ever tried to stop them.

They spoke to hard-nosed New Yorkers, who probably wouldn't have listened to them before 9/11, and they spoke to people from all over the world—Tibet, Martinique, Bangladesh, Jamaica Korea, Ghana, China, Switzerland. They ministered to construction workers, businessmen, and homeless people. So many people who had been traumatized by what had happened and were ready to talk to someone.

Ken was even interviewed by a reporter for *Time*

Magazine. As he answered her *reporter* questions, he also answered questions that went deeper. He presented the gospel to her through his answers and gave her much to reflect on about the beautiful nature of Jesus. Her photographer followed Ken around for the next half hour, taking pictures. Ken was also able to share with him and give him materials to read. (A picture of Ken walking the cross appeared in the November issue of *Time.*)

Early on, Ken had connected with a construction worker near his hotel that had come to the United States from Ireland. He was tall and thin and had on dirty coveralls and big work gloves. He seemed slightly awkward and embarrassed, but was mesmerized at the sight of a life-sized wooden cross.

Ken could tell this young Irishman really wanted to talk. They were on a break, so Ken explained to him about the person of Jesus and what had happened on the cross. The rest of the crew were silent and listening to every word. When their break was finished, Ken gave them all literature and left.

Every day, as Ken went out to minister, he would connect with this young man and talk to him for a few minutes. The day before Ken came back home, he noticed he and his crew were packing up. Ken asked him if they were finished, and he nodded his head and said, "I see you're still at it." Ken told him his work was almost complete and that he would be flying home the next day.

Ken then looked at him and said "I hope I had some impact on your life this week." He smiled broadly and said in his thick Irish accent, "That you did!" He told Ken he had read the material he had given him.

As they were getting ready to part, the young man pointed to the cross and blurted out, "Is that thing heavy?" Ken told him, no that it only weighed about forty pounds.

Then he said "I'd like to try it on my shoulder, if I might." Then and there, right on the corner of Broadway and 45th Street on Times Square, surrounded by thousands of people, this young man lifted the cross onto his shoulder.

He walked a few steps and stood there with it on his shoulder a couple of minutes. He finally put it down, grinned real big, shook hands with Ken, and said goodbye. But he had identified with Jesus and the cross and hopefully been changed forever.

Many people saw the cross that week and received literature that contained the life-changing gospel of Jesus Christ.

One thing we realized as we contemplated the last weeks of 2001 was that America needed the gospel in a greater way. The attacks on 9/11 had shaken America to its core and for a few weeks it seemed people were more serious and ready for changes in their lives. But as the weeks wore on, it was back to business as usual.

The world was still our mission field, but God was changing our emphasis back to America for a season. In the next years, we still traveled to foreign countries, but a new mission field opened up before us that we had never dreamed of. We were ready to meet that challenge and follow God as He led us.

*And then he (Jesus) told them, "Go into all the world
and preach the Good News to everyone."*
—Mark

Author's Note

As I look back on the places I have been able to visit and the things I have witnessed, I am amazed. God took a dairy farmer's daughter from North Carolina, plopped her down in Texas, and then had her marry a travelin' man. Adventure of this kind had been in my heart since I was a young girl. It was a dream come true and I am so thankful to have been able to fulfill this sense of adventure with a worthwhile and fulfilling direction.

There was indeed another reason for this love of travel and adventure. It is part of God's eternal plan that we reach out to others with the gospel of Jesus Christ. God spoke to me years ago to give my heart to the world. There are so many people to tell and so few people telling the Good News. As Jesus said in Matthew 9:37, the fields are ready for harvest, but the workers are few.

What is the message? That people can be saved from their guilt and shame. That they can have a new start in life and become a new creation. God meant for all of us to have a life of fulfillment and purpose, and then eternal life with Him. He wants to be a Father to us and lead us through this life here on earth—until we start our life with Him in Heaven.

I'm already working on a sequel to this story that will tell the next several years in our life and ministry together. I hope this story has blessed you and even entertained you. I would love to hear from you and receive your comments. I would also like to hear the story of your journey. If you have heard the call to go to the world to share the gospel, please share it with us. Go to Facebook page – ***Paradise Publications*** (Burleson, TX).

Quotes

Chapter 1: Spoken to Soviet Union leader Mikhail Gorbachev in regard to destroying the Berlin Wall. The speech was at the Brandenburg Gate near the Berlin Wall on June 12, 1987, commemorating the 750th anniversary of Berlin.

Chapter 2: From *The Explorer*

Chapter 3: From *Afraid? Of What?* This poem was written by E.H. Hamiliton, following the martyrdom of one of his colleagues, Jack Vinson in 1931. Mr. Vinson showed no fear of death to his Chinese captors. When they asked him, "Are you afraid?" he told them, "No, if you shoot, I go straight to heaven." They proceeded to shoot him. A young Chinese girl later related the events to Mr. Hamilton. Here is the poem in its entirety:

Afraid? Of what?
To feel the spirit's glad release?
To pass from pain to perfect peace,
The strife and strain of life to cease?
Afraid? Of that?

Afraid? Of what?
Afraid to see the Saviour's face,
To hear His welcome, and to trace,
The glory gleam from wounds of grace,
Afraid? Of that?

Afraid? Of what?
A flash - a crash - a pierced heart;
Brief darkness - Light - O Heaven's art!
A wound of His a counterpart!
Afraid? Of that?

Afraid? Of what?
To enter into Heaven's rest,
And yet to serve the Master blessed?
From service good to service best?
Afraid? Of that?

Afraid? Of what?
To do by death what life could not -
Baptize with blood a stony plot,
Till souls shall blossom from the spot?
Afraid? Of that?

Chapter 4: Quoting 2 Corinthians 2:16 NIV

Chapter 5: Missionary to South Africa, 1817

Chapter 6: Acts 14:22a (Phillips)

Chapter 7: An 18th Century evangelist who preached in England and America during the Great Awakening.

Chapter 10: Founder of the Salvation Army

Chapter 11: When God called him to walk with a life-sized cross across America.

Chapter 12: In 1807, Robert Morrison became the first

Protestant Missionary to China. The man asking him this question was the captain of the ship taking him to China.

Chapter 13: One of the five missionaries martyred in 1956 seeking to evangelize a hidden tribe in Ecuador.

Author's Note: Mark 16:15